The Making

of A Man

"My Cross to Bear"

Note for Librarians: A cataloguing record for this book is available from Library
and Archives Canada at www.collectionscanada.ca/amicus/index-e.html

Printed in Victoria, BC, Canada.

ISBN: 978-1-4251-9104-7 (sc)

*We at Trafford believe that it is the responsibility of us all, as both individuals
and corporations, to make choices that are environmentally and socially sound.
You, in turn, are supporting this responsible conduct each time you purchase a
Trafford book, or make use of our publishing services. To find out how you are
helping, please visit www.trafford.com/responsiblepublishing.html*

*Our mission is to efficiently provide the world's finest, most comprehensive
book publishing service, enabling every author to experience success.
To find out how to publish your book, your way, and have it available
worldwide, visit us online at www.trafford.com*

 www.trafford.com

North America & international
toll-free: 1 888 232 4444 (USA & Canada)
phone: 250 383 6864 ♦ fax: 250 383 6804 ♦ email: info@trafford.com

The United Kingdom & Europe
phone: +44 (0)1865 487 395 ♦ local rate: 0845 230 9601
facsimile: +44 (0)1865 481 507 ♦ email: info.uk@trafford.com

10 9 8 7 6 5 4 3 2 1

Contents

WHO AM I?

Who am I and why should you take the time to read this book. I am you:

This book is an attempt to help everyone, including myself, who has ever asked this important question to themselves; "Who Am I or "Why am I here?" Have you ever thought of life as never being what it seems to be? What I have found out in life is the things that we have gone through in life, can make or break us. The important thing here is what you do with the hand that you are dealt with? For example, I like many children, were born in this world, to a parent or parents that failed to accept their responsibilities. But the important lesson, written in this book is that we learn to understand the move of God, and not get so wrapped up in what man has or hasn't done to us, in this life; even if they are your parents. It's my hope, that after you finish reading this book, which you will find it within Christ Jesus, victory in your lives, and a need to help whoever you find to be in these similar situations. Remembering this, every person has their *"Cross to Bear"*: *"No cross, no crown"*.

Even though I Peter 2:5, 9-10 reads:

5 Ye also, as lively stones, are built up a spiritual house, and holy priesthood, to offer up spiritual sacrifices, acceptable to God by Jesus Christ
9 But ye are a chosen generation, a royal priesthood, an holy nation, a peculiar people; that ye should shew forth the praises of him who hath called you out of darkness into his marvelous light:
10 Which in time past were not a people, but are now the people of God: which had not obtained mercy, but now have obtained mercy.

We must understand that we don't always think, feel or believe these things to be true. I am living proof of that fact. It is this weakness in our lives; the not knowing who we truly are that puts us in the need of a Savior. All of us stand in need of the Lord in our lives, to fulfill the purposes in which we were created. I am a "Man of God". I am one who has seen his soul saved from self-destruction. One who has seen his marriage saved from divorce. I am he that has been given an opportunity to establish a wholesome relationship first with God, then my family. I am he that has total trust in God, to do His Will in me, according as He has purposed in His heart. With this in mind, all your questions can and will be answered. One of my toughest fights is the thought that I have towards my biological father. The irony here is that I teach my sons and other young men to love their fathers, even if they aren't around. I teach them that we are to honor our parents, despite what they have or haven't done. Our parents haven't sinned against us when they failed us; they have sinned against God. David said in the book of Psalm 51:1-5:

1 Have mercy upon me, O God, according to thy loving kindness: according unto the multitude of thy tender mercies blot out my transgressions.
2 Wash me thoroughly from mine iniquity, and cleanse me from my sin.
3 For I acknowledge my transgressions: and my sin is ever before me.
4 Against thee, thee only, have I sinned, and done this evil in thy sight: that thou mightest be justified when thou speakest,
5 Behold, I was shapen in iniquity; and in sin did my mother conceive me.

This, very well might be the prayer of all our estranged parents. Just remember though, all transgressors will answer to God. Let God's love heal all wounds.

I am Michael Linwood Jones Sr., the youngest son, of three boys, but I am older than all the girls, totaling six children. I was born to Dorothy Jean Parmer-Jones and Terry McArthur Jones, both of

Georgiana, Alabama. I was born in the city of brotherly love; known as Philadelphia, Pennsylvania. I was born on the 29th day of May 1964.

At this present time I am 38 years old, but in a few short months, three to be exact, I will be blessed to be 39 years of age. It is indeed a blessing and a pleasure to have reached this particular age, because many people had counted me out as a lost. I myself, had counted me out a time or two, but God allowed me to know that He created me for His own purpose. As a child, the Lord had allowed me to see a vision showing me what He was going to do within my life. He allowed me to know that I would be working in the area of evangelism, worldwide. I never knew how or when it would happen, but I know God is true to His Word. God lets us know that heaven and Earth will pass away, before His Word fails. This is why I am standing on His precious Word.

I myself am a father of seven children and a grandfather of three (two boys and a girl). I have five sons and two daughters. The only regret that I have is that all my children are not under the same roof, in which I now abide. It is important that we, parents, look after our children. We are to train them up in the way that they should go, in hopes that they won't depart from it. We are to work towards leaving an inheritance for our children and our children's children.

As a father, both to those under my roof, and to those living elsewhere, I realized my duties of teaching them (my children) the ways of the Lord. None of us are ever excused from God's command of training up my children, so I have purposed in my heart do this with every fiber of my being. This scripture can be found in Proverbs 22:6. It is my special duty, which is incumbent upon all parents, that we should teach our children diligently, and we should talk to them when we sit in the house, and when we walk by the way, when we lie down, and when we rise up. What is this thing that we should be teaching our children, it is the ways and Word of God? He commands us to do so, and so shall we perform that, which He has commanded us.

Throughout my children's lives, from time to time, I had an opportunity to share the Word of God with them. I pray that they themselves are teaching their children the Word of God. The command that was given to me as a parent, is the same command given to them. I have been blessed to see that my eldest son Michael is rearing his daughter, I believe in the admonition of the Lord. If it is not happening, I must still speak those things that are not as though they be, by faith.

I am a husband of one wife, for the past eight plus years. My wife Comisa, was born in 1972, and is the daughter of Calvin Thomas and the former Sandra Landry of Sunset, Louisiana. I am blessed to have her in my life, as my wife. It is not often that a man meets and marries a woman after only ten days. That's not the best part of it, God has allowed us to endure all the hardships, and still remain together regardless of what we had desired to do.

I am a Minister of the Gospel of Christ. Although I am a minister, I believe I have been chosen to work in the area of an evangelist. I was shown a vision of this at the age of about the age of sixteen, while living in Bridgeton, New Jersey. I have held on to that vision since then. I shared this vision with my brother Jeffery, some fifteen years ago, because he too will be working in the ministry. The thing that is so wonderful about God is, that we may not know how it is going to happen, but it will. As far as I know, Jeffery is not yet born again, but I believe God.

I am a member of Mt. Zion Missionary Baptist Church, Hinesville, Ga., where my pastor is Dr. M. L. Jackson. I am a Staff Sergeant, in the United States Army. I have been in the military for a total active duty period of fourteen years, eleven months and 14 days. I am eligible to be looked at on the Sergeant First Class Promotion board. I believe, by faith, I will be selected for the rank of Sergeant First Class this year. I had to change my attitude, mentally and spiritually in order to be in the right position for this promotion. While in the military, God has allowed me to receive three college degrees. I have a Bachelor of Religious Arts in Biblical Studies from Jacksonville Theological Seminary. I also have obtained Associate degrees in General Studies and Applied Sciences-Criminal Justice from Central Texas College.

As it is stated in the beginning of this book, obedience leads to deliverance. I really desired to be promoted from the rank of Staff Sergeant (now seven years), and allowed to prosper in all aspects of my life, even as my soul was to prosper. The key to that is my having the right attitude and my being obedient to the Will of God.

It is my goal to support the ministry in tithes and offering, working in the jail and prison ministries, and through supporting the pastor in whatever vision that God has given him. It is also my personal goal to open up a halfway house for former inmates and youths that are released from all types of correction facilities, all of which will offer them hope, spiritual guidance, and an opportunity to become productive citizens in their communities. I want to be able to house and educate them, to the point that they will be functionally sound, and self-supportive. I see them being able to give back to their perspective communities, and their deterring youths from a life of crime. This is just the tip of the iceberg, for what God has and will allow me to do, in His name.

Acknowledgments

"I am the way that I am today because of what happened to me in my past". This is a phrase that I oftentimes heard repeatedly from my wife Comisa, whom I thank very much for fighting for our marriage and family life. These words, which constantly cause me struggle, within my spiritual and natural life, have led me to constantly seek for answers from God.

My ministry as a preacher had seemingly come to an end, as well as my second marriage. My military career had peaked as far as it could go. Seemingly, I had done everything humanly possible to get promoted, but it never happened. Lastly and most importantly was my family life, which undoubtedly was seemingly ending in disaster. I then listened to the voice of God through a word from my pastor, "You haven't done what I told you to do, pay your tithes and trust God".

While in what seemed to be the worst pitfall of my life, my friend, Pastor Jackson encouraged me to hold on and trust God. A few weeks earlier I had spoken to him concerning a sermon that God had given me, concerning my trusting God and my not putting all my hope in man. I was so caught up in the things in which I was going through; I had forgotten what the message was. It wasn't until later, that I remembered the message. All of us need to be more loyal to God, rather than to man. This is where I went wrong. So here goes my life story from past to present, and we all will see how one is rewarded for either obedience or disobedience. Remember, the devourer will be rebuked, by God himself, because of your obedience to His Word. So remember to trust in the Lord, and lean not to thy own understanding.

Introduction:

So, you ask, this question, "What qualifies me to write this book?" I answer, Life. Because I am a human being, created and chosen by God, to do His will on Earth; I am entitled to use the gift of teaching, through this book, based on my life and the Word of God, given to me. I speak on many things that I have both lived and learned.

Like many, I too have been raped, abused, mistreated and felt alone. This is only the "tip of the iceberg". Because I have had my share of burdens, I am beginning to understand my own subheading of the title of this book, "My Cross to Bear". I understand the subject of "Wounds that have Healed", but having "Scars as reminders". I, just like many have the need of a "Right Way of Thinking". I have found myself asking God for "Peace to Be in My House".

One may ask why some of these words are in parenthesis, as if they have some significance to them, the reader. They do, for not only are the titles to sermons that I have preached, but they can attest to the dealings in which God has brought me through. It is hard for a person to accept any words that I have written in this book, solely based on the fact that, I, as an author have written it; especially because I am an unknown. But this doesn't make the events or words less important. My evidence evolves from the fact of knowing that God has taken me through these trials of life, from start to finish. Philippians 1:6-8 reads:

6 Being confident of this very thing, that he which hath begun a good work in you will perform it until the day of Jesus Christ:

7 Even as it is meet for me to think this of you all, because I have you in my heart; inasmuch as both in my bonds, and in the defense and confirmation of the gospel, ye all are partakers of my grace.

8 For God is my record, how greatly I long after you all in the bowels of Jesus Christ.

Remember, even if you don't feel or believe that God has begun a good work in you or your life's events, He still will perform that which He has predestined from your life. It is totally up to you, as to how you get there though. We all have our lives to live and our "crosses to bear".

Chapter One

How Did I Get To This Point In My Life

Oftentimes throughout my adult life I wondered why I was put here on earth. Feelings of despair, depression, confused and unnerved by my children, I look for answers from above. It seems as though there is no answer to be found. There are people in the world that feel just like me. I long for the assurance that God would smile and move towards me, but I assumed that He might be too selective to feel anything for me. I may even see Him as an unchanging, eternal spirit who lives far above the ever-changing winds of pain and emotion that blow in and out of my lives.

But that is not true of the God of the Bible. The Scriptures assures all road worn, dejected people, and everyone else, that He feels deeply for the most broken. He cannot be touched by our strengths, but only by our weaknesses. While God's character never changes, His affections do change. To know God is to affect Him. While God knew us, loved us, and chose us along with all His people in eternity past (Ephesians 1:3-6), He relates to us personally and presently in a very intimate way. He rejoices with us when we are happy, sorrows when we are sad, and grieves when we are bad. He has made Himself just that vulnerable to us. He has exposed His own heart to all of the loveless and heartless things that we do to Him. The Bible tells us that God can be:

- Pleased (Hebrews 11:5)
- Grieved and sorrowful (Genesis 6:6;Ephesians 4:30-32).
- Provoked and tested (Psalms 78:40-41).
- Burdened and wearied (Isaiah 43:24).
- Angered, agitated, and furious (Ezekiel 16:42-43).

Specifically, Ephesians 4:30-32 says, "Do not grieve the Holy Spirit of God, by whom you were sealed for the day of redemption. Let all bitterness, wrath, anger, clamor, and evil speaking be put away from you, with all malice. And be kind to one another, tenderhearted, forgiving one another, just as God in Christ forgave you."

The greatest evidence of His decision to make Himself vulnerable to us is found in the personal pains and sorrows of The One who with His own mind and heart revealed the Father to us. In the face of Jesus Christ, we find the face of God. He is the One who suffered for us so He could bring us to the Father. He loves us that much! It might be hard for us to personalize that kind of love when we know we are only one in a world of more than 5 billion people. But we need to keep in mind that it is we in which we are talking about. God does not have our limitations. He is not confined to human, one-at-a-time relationships. Rather, the One who made the world is able to relate intimately to as many of us at the same time as He desires.

How do we know God has that kind of capacity? We might come to that conclusion by reflecting on the size and complexity of the universe He created. Or we might consider the vast amounts of knowledge and information that finite people like ourselves can amass through the global Internet. Or we might simply trust the words of the One who said:

Are not two sparrows sold for a copper coin? And not one of them falls to the ground apart from your Father's will. But the very hairs of our head is also counting the tears, the moments of our fears, and the depth of the swirling waters threatening to engulf us.

If God knows us with this kind of knowledge, then we are never as alone as we feel. We are need without help. We are never out of the

Father's reach. Even though He might test our faith and our patience by not responding immediately in the way we want Him to, we can be are assured with a peace and confidence that can calm the turbulence within and lead to dramatic changes in us. To know God is to be affected by Him. Think for a moment about the people who have changed your life for the better. Maybe it was the teacher who inspired you to go for your dreams. Maybe it was the parent or grandparent whose words and hugs made you feel deeply loved. Maybe it was the neighbor who showed you by his example that any job worth having is worth doing well. Looking back, you can see that knowing these people changed your life.

What is true of these people will be even more of those who come to know God. No one can know Him without being changed by Him. Anyone who comes into God's presence will be touched and changed by the One who loves us enough to accept us as we are, but loves us too much to leave us that way. The apostle James described such a personal relationship with God like this:

Therefore submit to God. Resist the devil and he will flee from you. Draw near to God and He will draw near to you. Cleanse your hands, you sinners; and purify your hearts, you double-minded. Lament and mourn and weep! Let your laughter be turned to mourning and your joy to gloom. Humble yourselves in the sight of the Lord, and He will lift you up (4:7-10).

To know of God in this way means allowing our hearts to be broken by the things that break His heart. It means finding joy in the things that bring Him joy, discovering strength in His strength, and receiving hope in the assurance that nothing is too hard for him. It means finding a new lease on life in One who offers us forgiveness in exchange for our repentance, comfort in trade for our sorrow, and the promise of a world to come for our willingness to release our grip on this present one.

We are changed as we discover that to know God is to love Him. To love Him is to give Him first place in our hearts. Giving Him first place is to care about those He cares about, to love what He loves, to hate what He hates, and to join Him in the family business of redeeming broken lives. This is the kind of healthy relationship that God calls us to. But such maturity doesn't just happen. Sometimes a personal relationship with God remains a faint glimmer of what it was meant to be. Sometimes we stop short of the growth to which God call us.

Years ago, I had a pastor who spoke a word to me, while praying for me, that I would have the "Spirit of Job'. I didn't know much about Job, I was just glad to hear a Word from God, because I was wondering if I was put here on Earth just to suffer. What I did know was that in the end that Job was a successful and blessed man of God. I didn't get a full realization of all that he endured to reach the point of success; he suffered tremendously. The book of Job does discuss his ups and downs, i.e. dealing with his children, wife, and his doubtful friends, but through it all he remained faithful to God, unlike me.

As an adult, I look back over my life and wonder what happened in my life to get me to the point where I am today. Was it the sickness tat I endured as a baby? No, because the only part of that I remember is actually being rushed to the hospital and being put in an incubator around the age of 1 to 2 years of age. I could remember that vision as if it were yesterday. I remember being with my great grandmother in the projects in Alabama crawling up the sidewalk outside, and even the day she died. It was only that small glimpse of my childhood that I could remember, up to the ages of 3 or 4 years. Even when you or I can't remember the past, it shouldn't prevent us from living now, and shouldn't stop us from pressing towards the mark of the prize of the high calling of God in Christ Jesus.

But before I could move on in life, I had to deal with some issues; the enemy within.

Within me laid a desire to have a virgin. The desire to be someone's first sexual partner seemed to be of the uttermost importance. This desire within me was not of God, but could only be delivered from within me, by God.

If I wanted to be free, I had to be willing to challenge all the definitions of my masculinity. I had to fight against many of the things that most men would rather forget. Freedom would only come when I challenged myself; when I opened up and said things to myself that I might not have admitted to my wife, to my friends, or to my parents. It was time for me to confront the old issues in my life. These issues were the enemy of my soul.

The book of Romans 1:21-28, painted a scary picture of men who failed to deal with their enemy within themselves:

"21Because that, when they knew God, they glorified him not as God, neither were thankful; but became vain in their imaginations, and their foolish heart was darkened. 22 Professing themselves to be wise, they became fools, 23 And changed the glory of the uncorruptible God into an image made like to corruptible man, and to birds, and fourfooted beasts, and creeping things 24 Wherefore God also gave them up to uncleanness through the lusts of their own hearts, to dishonour their own bodies between themselves: 25 Who changed the truth of God into a lie, and worshipped and served the creature more than the Creator, who is blessed for ever. Amen. 26 For this cause God gave them up unto vile affections: for even their women did change the natural use into that which is against nature; 27 And likewise also the men, leaving the natural use of the woman, burned in their lust one toward another; men with men working that which is unseemly and receiving in themselves that recompense of their error which was meet. 28 And even as they did not like to retain God in their knowledge, God gave them over to a reprobate mind, to do those things which are not convenient...

These people may or may not have once known the Lord, but they decided not to glorify Him as God. His judgment was to turn them over to themselves! When we are left to our own selves, we may be surprised to know how corrupt we really are or can be. We may hide many things in us that we don't talk about. There are hidden things in us that we look down on others for, but we make sure that no one knows what is really on the inside of our heart. We know the evil that is lurking in the dark corners of our heart. The scary thing is that you never know when these things are going to rise up within us. When the right button is pushed, it allows your enemy within you to rear its ugly head. You may find yourself doing or wanting to do things that you felt you could never even have thought of.

Because you don't fully understand how many moral or emotional landmines are buried inside you, you may be vulnerable to erupt at any moment. The greatest and most lethal weapon that the enemy can ever challenged us with is ourselves. We are challenged in unique and special ways to help us to know who we are, despite our handicaps. When we don't have goals, it is easy for others to impose on us their ideas of who we are and are not, and of what we should and should not be doing. Anytime we don't know and understand our purpose, or who we were created to be, we become vulnerable to manipulation.

If you are not careful, you could have ended up like me, feeling that the power of God was unable or unwilling to change my situation. Here's a word of encouragement, found in the book of Romans 4:17, part b:

17 God "calleth those things which be not as though they were".

Why? He knows He has the power to make me become what He says I will be. He is not afraid to call me holy and blameless, even while I am I am still confused, in trouble and turmoil! I may have been guilty of inflicting domestic violence or mental abuse, but God says, "When I get through with him, he's going to be a deacon in the church, and I did become one". He didn't stop there; he made me a preacher, Praise God. I thank Him for blessing me and keeping me when I was in MY mess.

God has reserved a place for me, and "there isn't anyone who will be able to get in that place but me". Some of my enemies and friends thought that I wouldn't be there, but God said it will and is so; to the Glory of God. There were times when even I thought that I wouldn't be there.

God had to get me ready. I had to get ready before I could be in the place that God had for me. He has reserved a place for me. When I was in my darkest sin, God had His angels watching over me. When I may have wanted to slap my wife around and boasted about how I wasn't going to church, or preach God's Word again, God protected me from myself. He knew exactly how He was going to pull that bitterness out of me and bring me to my knees. I am a miracle. God allowed me to share that message in Kuwait, "Looking at a Miracle", on New Years Eve. 2002.

If God had dealt with me according to my sins, I would be dead. But God is merciful. He was determined to turn me around and place in a position where he could minister to me. Because I belong to God, He went to extreme measures to get me away from people, the cliques and clubs, bars, society and any other kind of entanglement that would have hindered me from hearing His voice. But when I decided to listen, when He called, he arranged things in my life so He could have me to Himself completely.

Chapter Two

My Remonstration With God

Many times in life we have our views on different issues concerning us and we must find a way to express those issues without them become overwhelming for us. As aforementioned in chapter one, I discussed a prophecy spoken to me by Apostle Robert L. Howard, pastor and founder of the Word of God Church Incorporated, in Washington D. C. He spoke of a "Spirit of Job", which he pronounced to me as coming from God. I'm referring to this as I look back at the entire 7th chapter of Job, in the Holy Bible. It tells how job remonstrates with God. In order to understand this chapter, one needs to understand what remonstration means in order to follow where I am taking you. I want to illustrate to God my earnest opposition or views concerning the life or hand that has been given me. In order and all fairness to God, as if I can be fair within myself, I must also realize one thing, and that is the mistakes that I have made in my life have a large part concerning the successes or failures in my life.

As I sit here, I wonder if I just received that spoke word from this Man of God as being true, and therefore my life is now full of grief. If so I must also except within and myself that this too will pass the end I, and all those around me will be victorious and prosperous as Job was. He suffered and was criticized by those closest to him, but he never gave up on God, or accused God of any wrong doings.

Job says in the 1st verse of chapter 7:1-3:

1 Is there not an appointed time to man upon earth? Are not his days also like the days of as a hireling? 2 As a servant earnestly desireth the shadow, and as a hireling looketh for the reward of his work; 3 so am I made to possess months of vanity, and wearisome nights are appointed to me.

I have questioned many times throughout my life, "How long am I going to have a life like this one?" Are these individual or individuals a part of my life here just to make me suffer or to help to prove me? It is easy to except this "Spirit of Job" being pronounced on my life if I considered the general condition of man upon the earth according to biblical scriptures. It reads, "He is of few days, and full of trouble". Every man must die shortly, and every man has some reason (more or less) to desire to die shortly; and therefore why should you impute it to me as so heinous a crime that I should wish to die shortly? According to my Matthew Henry commentary, this is what Job was saying to God, "It stated that Job asked God not to mistake his desires of death, as if he thought the time appointed of God could be anticipated: no Job new that this time was fixed."

For many persons like me, the question seems to be, "How long will this suffering go on? With all the promises of victory in the end, overwhelming blessings in my life to come, it seems unrealistic when you go through the here and now. It isn't that I don't believe that I am an over comer in life, by faith in Christ Jesus, it's just seeing what is actually is before me, that's seemingly trying to overtake me in the present. I have been undergoing such a spiritual battle within myself for well over 15 years. So, have months of vanity, as Job phrases it, and wearisome nights finally taken its toll, or has God allowed this to awaken my spiritual awareness, in order for me to understand that He really is in control of my life? If so, when will my change come? I realize that all things work together for them that love the Lord. I also realize that if we don't suffer with Him, we won't reign with Him, but why doesn't God hinder us form making these mistakes in the first place. The answer came before I could finish typing the question. God has created us as beings with the power of choice of right and wrong.

In the fourth verse Job states:

4 When I lie down, I say, when shall I arise, and the night be gone? And I am full of tossings to and fro unto the dawning of the day".

It seems evident that if you have had a relationship with God before and gone away from Him, there will never be any true peace without Him in your life. Before I really even knew anything about Jesus Christ, He had already made plans for my life. I came to that realization at least ten or more years ago, after seeing a vision come true before my very eyes. When I was about the age of 13-16, I saw the face of a man that I learned later as Elder Smith, from the Word of God Church, in Washington D.C. The key here is that then I was about twenty-six years of age when it actually came to fruition. I also saw my brother and I evangelizing the gospel around the world. I shared this vision or dream, as you will, with him well over fifteen years ago. Throughout my life I have been tossed to and fro with this idea because of which I saw myself to be, and because of what we had been through in my lifetime. Even at this very moment, I am wrestling with the fact of being the man that God would have me to be, verses the things the things that I have to deal with in order to get to the place in God, which I need to be.

Verse 11 in the same book of Job helps me to realize the importance of speaking my mind to God. I want God to realize that I will not refrain my mouth from speaking the anguish of my spirit. I will complain in the bitterness of my soul. I too oftentimes would rather be dead than continue to face a life such as this one. As Job does, so do I ask?

17 what is man, that thou shouldest magnify him? And that thou shouldest set thine heart upon him? 18 And that thou shouldest visit him every morning, and try him every moment: 19 how long wilt thou not depart from me, nor let me alone till I swallow down my spittle? 20 I have sinned; what shall I do unto thee, O thou preserver of men? Why hast thou set me as a mark against thee, so that I am a burden to myself? 21 And why dost thou not pardon my transgression, and take away mine iniquity? For now shall I

sleep in the dust; and thou shalt seek me in the morning, but I shall not be.

These are words well written concerning the sentiments of my heart. Is it really necessary for me to continuously suffer because of whom God has made me to be? There are times when I can't stand myself. I hate the very vision of myself that I see in the bathroom mirror. I must remember the hands of God have wonderfully made me. Can one really remonstrate with God, and get his point across, and still be in good standings with God.

Chapter Three

A Right Way Of Thinking

Thoughts and groupings of words seem to form ideas in your mind, which will lead one to the thinking process. So, what does this have to do with anything? To think, or to become involved in the thinking process, states that one needs to form or have something in the mind. You need to have as an intention or to have as an opinion, a thought. You could regard something as an opinion, or consider reflecting on a particular idea. How did the way I pictured things in my own mind affect the way I turned out at this particular point in life. Who taught me how to think, or who knows what the right way of thinking truly is?

Thinking is a process that forms in the mind. In the mind, elements or a complex of elements in an individual results in feelings, perceptions, thoughts, will, and the reasoning process. All of these processes happen, but it is important that the right way of thinking is most evident in our lives. The Word of God lets us know in the book of Romans 12:2-3, which discusses how to think and the benefits of thinking right:

2 And be not conformed to this world: but be ye transformed by the renewing of your mind, that ye may prove what is that good, and acceptable, and perfect, will of God. 3 For I say, through the grace given unto me, to every man that is among you, not think of

himself more highly than he ought to think; but to think soberly, according as God hath dealt to every man the measure of faith.

The most powerful example of the thought process is found in the book of Philippians 2:5-11, which dealt with having the mind of Christ Jesus. Verses 5 through 11 read:

5 Let this mind be in you, which was also in Christ Jesus: 6 Who, being in the form of God, thought it not robbery to be equal with God: 7 But made himself of no reputation, and took upon him the form of a servant, and was made in the likeness of men: 8 And being found in fashion as a man, he humbled himself, and became obedient unto death, even the death of the cross. 9 Where forth God also hath highly exalted him, and given him a name above every name; 10 That at the name of Jesus every knee should bow, of things in heaven, and things in earth, and things under the earth; 11 And that every tongue should confess that Jesus Christ is Lord, to the glory of God the Father.

God has just given me a revelation on the importance of the thoughts of the mind, and the strength of our will. The scriptures illustrate how powerful a man's thoughts are. The phrase "every knee should bow, and every tongue should confess", shows us that it is possible that someone's mind, will, and thought processes will be at place to refuse Christ even after knowing who He is and what He has done for us a Savior of our sins. It has been a long time since I last written done my thoughts.

As I read the preceding paragraph, I felt that I have been given a scriptural answer that is not only true, but also biblically based, concerning why I am going why I am going through the different trials and tribulations in my life. In the book of James 4:1-7, speaks of the key element of man's failure, **lust**. Verse 1 says,

"From whence come wars and fightings among you? Come they not hence, even of our lusts that war in your members? 2 Ye lust, and have not: ye kill, and desire to have, and cannot obtain; ye fight and war; yet ye have not, because ye ask not. 3 ye ask, and receive not, because ye ask amiss, that ye may consume it upon your lusts.

4 Ye adulterers and adulteresses, know ye not that the friendship of the world is the enemy of God. 5 Do ye think that the scripture saith in vain, the spirit that dwelleth in us lusteth to envy? 6 but he giveth more grace. Wherefore he saith, God resisteth the proud, but giveth grace to the humble. 7 Submit yourselves therefore to God. Resist the devil, and he will flee from you.

It is amazing how God answers our questions. We have to be willing to receive the answers the feedback from Him without resolution. Verse 3, of St. James 4:1, hits home best of all. Many times in my life I desired things that were not good for me, for example, like King David, someone else's wife. I desired to have this woman at my beckoning call, only not to obtain her. The majority of the time when I saw her, I burned on the inside, wanting her to make love to me, and for her to want me as much as I wanted her. I told her oftentimes if her husband hurt her, I would hurt him, but God stepped in and helped me to understand that she didn't belong to me. I had to submit myself to God, and resist the devil, in order that he would flee from me.

I like how God does things, I was looking up a particular definition for the word remonstration, and I found out that there was no further need to question God, just obey his commandments and live. In doing so, I can live a prosperous life in Him. So, in the short of it, this chapter of my life is over. However, let's not forget, there will be times in our life when we will need a spiritual checkup. David wrote in Psalms 139:23-24:

23 "Search me, O God, and know my heart; test me and know my anxious thoughts. 24 See if there is any offensive way in me, and lead me in the way everlasting."

Just as a doctor points out signs of your heart and sickness during a physical checkup, the Holy Spirit will show you the condition of your heart. He can use Scripture and circumstances, among other things, to do it. And when he does, as when we receive our report from the doctor, along with signs of health, we may receive some bad news.

The good news is that God changes the hearts of men. God is interested most of all in the condition of your heart. In Acts 13:22 God testifies that in David he found a man after his own heart one whom he could count on to "do everything I want him to do". Would God find you to be such a man?

The development of a strong Christian character is the development of a man after God's own heart. Our character is who we are when no one is looking and what we are willing to stand for when someone is looking. Character is who we are striving to be and what we can be trusted with.

Integrity of character occurs when there is consistency between our actions and our inner convictions over time. Strong Christian character results from both human effort and divine intervention. It is the work of God as you relate to him in love. Strong Christian character is the result of our heart's desires to obey God. In developing a strong Christian character in our heart, in order to obey God, we must understand the heart of man according to the word of God. When we understand how thoughts enter the mind, which then enter the heart, we will know why we do or don't the things we that we do.

In reading and studying other books, I came across a wonderful section that dealt with the qualities of good character. There are many different qualities of character. The eight qualities of good character that will be introduced to you which are found in the person that God uses are holiness, a pure heart, a contrite heart, the fear of God, faithfulness, obedience, seeking and loving God, and being a servant of the Lord.

Just as the prophet Isaiah saw God seated on a throne, high and exalted with angels flying about, calling to one another in the book of Isaiah 6:3:

3 "Holy, holy, holy is the Lord Almighty; the whole earth is full of his glory."

I can see why Isaiah immediately cried out in despair because he recognized his sinfulness in the presence of a holy God. I too had to recognize where I was in the Lord. I saw how my wrong way of thinking led to wrong actions, resulting to sin. We know that the wages of sin is death, but the gift of God is eternal life.

Let's try to understand what and how these eight qualities of good character mean, and how they can affect our walk with Jesus. Holiness means "to be set apart and separate." We are to be separate from all that stains our world and dirties our lives, frees us from all sinful thoughts, destructive emotions, unclean images, impure motives, and questionable activities.

I have found out that I can't make myself holy. I can become holy only through the power of Christ and the working of the Holy Spirit in my life. Only through a pure and clean life, I will reveal to the world the reality of holiness through my life. Isaiah 35:8 states that God is building a highway of holiness that the wicked cannot travel.

And an highway shall be there, and a way, and it shall be called The way of holiness: the unclean shall not pass over it; but it shall be for those: the wayfaring men, though fools shall not err therein.

God desires that your life and mine be that highway, the road over which others may be drawn to Christ, the road over which God may bring revival to our land. All the prayers, sacrifices, and pleadings with God will not bring revival until we take seriously our holiness.

An impure heart and mind that fail to acknowledge sin are barriers to effectively praying and seeking the Lord. If we choose to fill our minds with pornography, violence, immorality, hatred, promiscuity, and self-centeredness and call it entertainment, God will not hear our prayers.\

A PURE HEART

A pure heart is the next quality needed. The word pure means "to be singular in substance, without any imperfections or impurities." A pure heart is one solely committed to Christ first and foremost. Proof of this fact can be found in St Matthew 10:37-39. St. Matthew 5:8 tells us that:

8 "Blessed are the pure in hear: for they shall see God."

The word sincere is closely associated with purity. It comes from the Latin phrase sine cere meaning "without wax." Wax was often used to cover or fill in cracks in pottery so that it could then be sold as undamaged. Under the test of fire, the wax would melt and reveal himself to us so we can see him clearly, we must approach him with "clean hands and a pure heart". Psalms 24:4-5 states;

4 He that hath clean hands and a pure heart; who hath not lifted up his soul unto vanity, nor sworn deceitfully. 5 He shall receive the blessing from the Lord, and righteousness from the God of His salvation.

It is not our responsibility to judge the other man. I Samuel 16:7 read:

7 But the Lord said unto Samuel, Look not on his countenance, or on the height of his stature; because I have refused him: for the lord seeth not as man seeth; for man looketh on the outward appearance, but the Lord looketh on the heart.

God searches the heart and try the reins (Jeremiah 17:10).

10 I the Lord search the heart, I try the reins, even to give every man according to his ways, and according to the fruit of his doings.

A CONTRITE HEART

Contrite means to be "humble and repentant before God, 2 crushed by a sense of guilt and sin. In one way we are responsible for how we come before God. In another way, God will bring us to the edge of brokenness through our circumstances. Part of a covenant love relationship involves God's helping us to repent when we need to, but it still remains an act of our will. The prodigal son was not prevented from leaving the security of his father's house (Luke 15:11-32). His father allowed him the freedom to choose. But after the son came to the humiliating realization of where his decisions had led him, he repented and humbly returned to his father to ask forgiveness. His father ran to meet him, rejoicing in his return.

A wonderful lesson that we can learn in life is following God's example. God can take a heart once hardened and rebellious and use circumstances to make it moldable and submissive. Without brokenness we become indifferent to God and to the needs of others. A proud heart exalts itself and promotes independence from God. This is sin. The remedy for sin is clearly repentance. David's heart cry, found in Psalm 51, still describes what men today feel when they repent their sin and asks God to revive and refresh their relationship with him. I find myself needing to pray this particular prayer.

Psalm 51:1-5, 9-12

1 Have mercy upon me, O God, according to they lovingkindness: according unto the multitude of they tender mercies blot out my transgressions. 2 Wash me thoroughly from mine iniquity, and cleanse me from my sin. 3 For I acknowledge my transgressions; and my sin is ever before me. 4 Against thee, thee only, have I sinned, and done this evil in thy sight: that thou mightest be justified when thou speakest, and be clear when thou judgest. 5 Behold, I was shapen in iniquity; and in sin did my mother conceive me.

8 Hide thy face from my sins, and blot out all mine iniquities. 10 Create in me a clean heart, O God; and renew a right spirit within me. 11 Cast me not away from thy presence; and take not thy holy spirit from me. 12 Restore unto me the joy of thy salvation; and uphold me with thy free spirit.

FEAR OF GOD

There are two kinds of fear that will be discussed in this section. There is the FEAR that Satan offers us, False Evidence Appearing Real, and the reverential fear towards God. Satan often times presents with false evidence that is convincing enough to appear real in our lives. We must understand what Jesus said to the Pharisees in St John 8:44:

44 Ye are of your father the devil, and the lusts of your father ye will do. He was a murderer from the beginning, and abode not in the truth, because there is not truth in him. When he speaketh of his own; for he is a liar, and the father of it.

Satan will sell you a bad bag of goods. Be sure that you don't buy into them, for the end of them is destruction.

The second and most important kind of fear is the fear of God. Fear brings a sense of awe and reverence toward God. Sometimes biblical fear can also refer to terror or dread when factoring God's judgment. Fearing God is part of walking in his ways, loving him and serving him with all our hearts as we observe his commands. Deuteronomy 10:12-13 states:

12 And now, Israel, what doth the Lord thy God require of thee, but to fear the Lord thy God, to walk in all his ways, and to love him, and to serve the Lord thy God with all thy heart and with all thy soul, 13 To keep the commandments of the Lord, and his statutes, which I command thee this day for thy good?

Too often we are more afraid of men than we are of God. Most men dread being ridiculed by others. Jesus warned, "Do not be afraid of those who kill the body but cannot kill the soul. Rather be afraid of the One who can destroy both soul and body in hell." (St Matthew 10:28)

A lack of fear of God demonstrates a lack of understanding of who God is and what he is able to do. We as Christians display a lack of fear towards God when we continually use God's name in vain, deliberately sin, expecting God to forgive us, view worship, prayer, tithing, studying God's Word, and commitment to the church as options for the Christian and approach God in worship with a flippant attitude. Lacking the true fear of God will allow you to be in this state spiritually.

St Matthew 10:18-20

And he said unto them, I beheld Satan as lightning fall from heaven. 19 Behold, I give unto you power to tread on serpents and scorpions, and over all the power of the enemy: and nothing shall by any means hurt you. 20 Notwithstanding in this rejoice not, that the spirits are subject unto you; but rather rejoice, because your names are written in heaven.

Satan was rendered powerless as the disciples stepped forth in obedience to the task Christ had given them We must be wise to Satan's methods (fear - false evidence appearing real), but fear is to be reserved for the one who has the rights to our lives.

FAITHFULNESS

The word faithful is linked to a promise: "Be faithful, even to the point of death, and I will give you the crown of life" (Revelation 2:10). Faithfulness is a lifelong goal. It is persevering to the end. Faithfulness is remaining true to the Lord and his Word through discouragement and difficulty as well as joy and success. Anything short of finishing the race is to be disqualified, and everyone who crosses the finish line is a winner.

God is searching for faithful men. He is searching for men he can trust to intercede on behalf of our nation. God is looking for men he can trust with God-sized tasks (Ezekiel 22;30). Will you be that man? Will his eyes rest on you or pass over you? Will he be able to say, "have you considered so and so?"

You may have been faithful. You may have stumbled in the race and are limping along the sidelines. Forgiveness and restoration are available for those who recognize their failures and repent of them. A life of faithfulness begins with the first step of obedience and continues one step at a time. Measure your faithfulness by applying this principle to your faithfulness to your family, friends, self, and employer, You will find it harder to be faithful to God if faithfulness is not a part of what you are in your other relationships

Be faithful, even to the point of death, and I will give you the crown of life" (Revelation 2:10)

OBEDIENCE

The apostle John wrote, "This love for God: to obey his commands. And his commands are not burdensome" (1 John 5:3). Many have rightly said that it is impossible for a man who loves God to say, "No, lord," because if Christ is truly our Lord, we cannot refuse him.

Obedience is submission to the instructions of an authority. Our obedience to Christ's commands is proof to God and to everyone watching us that Christ indeed is Lord of our lives. The act of baptism for a new Christian is the first act of obedience I response to the commands of Jesus Christ. I Samuel 15:22-23 tells us:

22 And Samuel said, Hath the Lord as great delight in burnt offerings and sacrifices, as in obeying the voice of the Lord? Behold, to obey is better than sacrifice, and to hearken than the fat of rams. 23 For rebellion is as the sin of witchcraft, and stubbornness is as iniquity and idolatry. Because thou hast rejected the word of the Lord, he hath also rejected thee from being king.

God doesn't want us just to give money to the church. God isn't looking to see how many hours we spend witnessing. It doesn't really matter how much we feel we had to give up to follow Christ. God wants to see if we have truly heard him. He wants to see us obey.

SEEKS AND LOVES GOD

God's Word says, "For thou shalt worship no other god: for the Lord, whose name is Jealous, is a jealous God." God not only demands our complete loyalty, but he also deserves it. God desires to be found by those who are seeking him. God longs to reveal himself to his people and share the blessings he has waiting for us. Even more, God wants to commune with us in a reciprocating love relationship.

One paradox in the Christian life is that we must seek God with our whole heart in order to find him, yet it is God who causes us to want to seek him in the first place. Jeremiah 29:11-12 describes the special relationship and promise God has provided for us. "For I know the plans I have for you, declares the Lord, plans to prosper you and not to harm you, plans to give you hope and a future. Then you will call upon me and come and pray to me, and I will listen to you.

God sets in motion his plans and his purposes for you, and then you will find in your heart a desire to seek after him. "No one can come to me unless the Father who sent me draws him (John6:44). It sounds so simple because it is, and yet all the complexity of God surrounds and enfolds that relationship. Love is the key. "We love (God) because he first loved us. If anyone says, "I love God", yet hates his brother, he is a liar... Whoever loves God must also love his brother (I John 4:19-21). God's love leaves no room for hatred of anyone. God loves them too and we cannot love God and hate the very ones he loves.

It is easier for us to love those whom God loves if we allow God to love through us. However, if we are disobedient, if we are choosing to serve ourselves, and our biases against others, then we are divided. "No servant can serve two masters. Either he will hate the one land love the other, or he will be devoted to the one and despise the other", (Luke 16:13). Not only is it difficult, but also resentment is bound to set in as the servant fails to serve either one adequately. Where does your devotion lie?

Chapter Four

A New Beginning

It is now 0727 a.m., February 9, 2002. I am saved by the grace of God, and I have the mind and the ability within to serve God. I repented of my sins, and I am following Romans 12:1-2, where Paul states,

"1 I BEESEECH you therefore, brethren, by the mercies of God that ye present your bodies a living sacrifice, holy acceptable unto God, which is your reasonable service. 2 And be not conformed to this world: but be ye transformed by the renewing of your mind, that ye may prove what is that good, and acceptable, and perfect, will of God."

It feels so good serving the Lord sincerely, and examining my thoughts, deeds, and actions on a daily basis to ensure that I am in compliance to His Word.

The Men's Fellowship is getting together today and I really want to attend, but I have my three sons to take care of. My wife has reserve duty obligations today. Prayerfully, I'll be able to make the 11 am leaders meeting. Working in the ministry is a wonderful thing, and seeing the blessings of God unfold before me, is even better. As a testimony to myself, and those who may read this book, God has strengthened my marriage, my relationship with my children, and stretched my finances beyond belief.

Time has come and gone since I last wrote in this book, depicting my life. My marriage and life had seemingly turned around for the better, but now here is a new twist, challenge or trial, if you may, I'm getting a divorce. It is now May 27, 2002, and I'm dealing with a physical affliction known as a severe acid reflux, which has put me in the position of having three surgeries and four dilations, all in which did nothing to make me better. As the title in this chapter reads, "A New Beginning", I never anticipated one such as the one that I'm about to face, alluding back to the discussion about our getting a divorce.

According to the agreement between my wife and me, I will be keeping all three of the boys. We will share joint custody of the children. Because I am preparing to deploy to Kuwait, she will be keeping the children with her, until I return. This new beginning of sorts is an attempt to alter my eldest son Tony's behavior, which would seemingly harmonious setting for all involved in this family. In my view, my wife's desire to allow my children to freely express themselves has caused them to lose their minds. They have become disrespectful and disobedient towards anyone in authority. My wife and I can't seem to agree on the levels of self-expression and freedoms, in which the children should have. They don't fully understand the importance of being responsible for their actions, so I feel she has set them up for future failure in life. They are to young to be given the responsibility of making decisions in their lives, such as what they will eat, drink, or what they do and don't want to do. I feel as parents, we are the ones responsible for making those types of decisions for them.

We also have a difference in opinion on what our roles are in this house. I feel that it is my responsibility to run our home. My wife feels that she should have more to say than she does. Some decisions that were made between the two of us have been very costly. I am the head of this household, whether she believes it or not and I will not accept anything else. I have accepted this responsibility without question, and I will not allow my wife to deter me from that responsibility. I love my wife very much, but I can't and won't allow her to continue to disrupt the order in which my home is supposed to run. We have come to an agreement that it is necessary for her to leave and allow me to rear m son's as God has given me the sever ability to do. My wife means well in her heart, but her methods have led my children to total disarray, behaviorally. I can't stand by and see my son's go in the wrong direction. I will not continue to argue with y wife on the issues of how my family will be run. Most importantly, neither she nor my son's will continue to disrespect me in this home. Equally important, I will not disrespect her or my children, while upholding the responsibility that God has bestowed on me.

I feel that this new beginning and change in my life will finally enable me to focus more on my God given mission here on earth. I have been given vision to build a home for ex-cons, which affords them an opportunity for living, and for them to become productive citizens. This will also allow me to work in this area of ministry that I feel that I am directed to work in. I will be able to teach my son's about life and its consequences resulting form the decisions that we may make in life. I have come to learn that no one owes us anything in life, and it's a hard and painful lesson to learn. My wife and I will remain friends throughout this process, and it is our intention to be equally involved in the lives of our children.

For the most part, we will both make decisions for their upbringing; we just can't seem to do it under the same roof. Our decision to divorce could not come at a worse time in my life. My health seems to be keeping me down, and occasionally causing me to be hospitalized. My son's are seemingly in a disarray, along with our spiritual life being at an all-time low. We really need God to intervene, like yesterday. This trying period should and will afford us the opportunity to seek God as to what He has for us to do, and how to accomplish whatever He has before us. I am at peace with the decision that I have made. My wife on the other hand, wants to stay together now, but I don't see it working out for everyone concerned. Maybe someday God will allow us to come back together; who but God only knows.

As we all know, the Satan is a liar and the Father of lies. Although we did do separation agreement in May 2002, the Lord never allowed us to go against His Word. See, what the Satan and we needed to know is what the scriptures tell us in the St Matthew 19:3-9:

3 The Pharisees, also came unto him, tempting him, and saying unto him, Is it lawful for a man to put away his wife for every cause? 4 and he answered and said unto them, Have ye not read, that he which made them at the beginning made them male and female, 5 And said, For this cause shall a man leave father and mother, and shall cleave to his wife: and they twain shall be one flesh? 6 Wherefore they are no more twain, but one flesh. What therefore God hath joined together, let not man put asunder. 7 They say unto him, Why did Moses then command to give a writing of divorcement, and to put her away? 8 He saith unto them, Moses because of the hardness of your hearts suffered you to put away your wives: but from the beginning it was not so. 9 And I say to you, Whosoever shallput away his wife, except it be for fornication, and shall marry another, committeth adultery: and whoso ever marrrieth her which is put away doth commit adultery.

One has to understand this one important fact, Moses was the Lawgiver, but God is the Creator of the man who gave the laws. My wife and I came to the understanding like Peter did in Acts 5:29, when Peter and the other apostles answered and said, We ought to obey God rather than man. Another important fact is that it is easy to give up, but it takes hard work and endurance to win the fit. Anything worth having is worth fighting for, and our family is worth fighting for.

Because we chose to obey God rather than man, He has restored our marriage and our home. By no means am I saying the fight is over, or the battle is won. What I am saying is that with Christ in us we have the victory over every work of Satan, as long as trust, depend and lean on Him and not ourselves. We realize that in order for this marriage to work, it won't be by our power or might, but by His Spirit saith the Lord of Host. Yes there are marriage seminars, pastoral counseling's, and even advice from family and friends, but the best answer is to obey the Word of God; we are.

ANOTHER OPPORTUNITY

I thank the Lord for another day of life. If it had not been for the Lord on my side, where would I be? I have been given another day and another chance to give Him praise, honor and glory. I have made it back from Kuwait with a renewed mind to serve God, through the serving my family in love. I didn't have a full understanding of what it meant to serve God with all my heart, soul and mind. As men and women of God, we have to put on the "Spiritual Apparel", which God has equipped us with. We should have put on the new man, as it is stated in the book of Colossians 3:10-14, which states:

10 And have put on the new man, which is renewed in knowledge after the image of him that created him:

11 Where there is neither Greek nor Jew, circumcision nor uncircumcision, Barbarian, Scythian, bond not free: but Christ is all, and in all.

12 Put on therefore, as the elect of God, holy and beloved, bowels of mercies, kindness, humbleness of mind, meekness, longsuffering;

13 Forbearing one another, and forgiving one another, if any man have a quarrel against any: even as Christ forgave you, so also do ye.

14 And above all these things put on charity, which is the bond of perfectness.

15 And let the peace of God rule in your hearts, to the which also ye are called in one body; and be ye thankful.

It took this significant event in my life to happen, in order for me to get on the right road with Christ Jesus. Jesus is true to His Word, when he says that He'll never leave thee or forsake thee, in the book of Hebrews, the thirteenth chapter and the 5th verse. We turn our backs on Jesus.

After I learned the necessity of allowing the word of Christ dwell in me richly, in all wisdom, and by teaching and admonishing one another in psalms and hymns and spiritual songs, singing with grace in my heart to the Lord, I then began to understand how to have the mind of Christ Jesus. The key to all of this is to remember that, whatsoever that I do in word or deed, I need to do it all in the name of the Lord Jesus, giving thanks to God and the Father by him. Then and only then would the rest of Colossians 3:18-25 become possible in my life.

Not knowing why this particular section was entitled "Another Opportunity", I found out the significance of it following a conversation with my eldest son Michael. He called me about 1020 p.m. He begun to apologize for it being so late, and for him waking me up, because I was asleep at the time he called. He really needed to talk, as a father does with his son. As I begun to listen, I was able to hear him and feel his pain. For I have been in similar situations that he is now facing as a father and a man. Being in an uncertain state, can cause you sleepless nights and worrisome days; days full of trouble.

But the great thing about all that happen was, I was given another opportunity to teach him correctly in the areas of life, which I had once misled him in. Because I myself was unseasoned, or lacking in wisdom, I fed him negative knowledge, which would have been counter-productive for his growth in life. My relationship with father was revived because of obedience to God through forgiveness. Now he will have an opportunity to have a relationship with his grandfather that he wouldn't have had, had I not been given another opportunity to correct the lessons taught to him, earlier in life. We can ill-afford to send out negative messages based on what we have experienced with people. It is up to each individual person to be able to develop their own opinions of the persons that they are dealing with for themselves.

There are two words that should have been discussed earlier, in this section of the book. The words are *"another opportunity"*. The word *another,* according to Webster's Ninth Collegiate Dictionary means: 1: different or distinct from the one first considered 2: some other 3: being one more in addition to one or more of the same kind: new. The other word is *opportunity*, which means: 1: a favorable juncture of circumstances 2: a good chance for advancement or progress.

After being tried in the fire of my own heart, and seeing life as it truly is, as God has allowed me to understand, I was able to have a different favorable attitude towards my father, which allowed us an opportunity for progress as father and son. There are things in life that we are allowed to experience, that will leave a bad taste in your mouth or heart, but one must be able to see it as God sees it. When God says in the book of Romans 8:28: And we know that all things work together for good to them that love God, to them who are the called according to *his* purpose, we should be more at ease knowing God is in control of our lives. This is easier for me to say now, looking back at where God has brought me.

I could not have allowed this opportunity passed me by, and not shared the good news about the process of sowing and reaping, when it comes to tithing and in living life. I had *another opportunity*, after hearing all that he said he was going through to share with him the process of sowing and reaping. Let me take the time and share with you the Word of God concerning sowing and reaping, according to Galatians 6:7-10. And it reads:

7 Be not deceived; God is not mocked: for whatsoever a man soweth, that shall he also reap. 8 For he that soweth tohis flesh shall of the flesh reap corruption; but he that soweth to the Spirit shall of the Spirit reap life everlasting. 9 And let us not be weary in well doing: for in due season we shall reap, if we faint not. 10 As we have therefore opportunity, let us do good unto all *men,* especially unto them who are of the household of faith.

So what does all that mean to you? There is a spiritual and natural way of looking at these particular verses. Let's see what the Matthew Henry Commentary says about these verses. On page 680, Roman number V, it states in verse 7 the following:

Here is a caution to take heed of don't mock God, or deceiving yourselves, by imagining that he can be imposed upon by mere pretensions or professions. You shouldn't entertain any vain hopes of enjoying life's rewards, while neglecting your spiritual or natural duties as a child of God. The apostle here supposes that many are apt to excuse themselves from the work of religion, and especially the more self-denying and chargeable parts of it, though at the same time they may make a show and profession of it. But he assures them that this, their folly, for though hereby they may possibly impose upon others, yet they do but deceive themselves if they think to impose upon God, who is perfectly acquainted with their hearts as well as actions, and He can't be deceived, so He will not be mocked.

Next we must realize that according to how we behave ourselves now, so will our account be in the great day. Our present time is seed-time. In the other world there will be a great harvest, and as the husbandman reaps in the harvest according as he has sown seedness, so we shall reap then as we sow now. In verse 8, we notice that there are two sorts of seedness, sowing to the flesh and sowing to the Spirit; and so accordingly will the reckoning be hereafter: if we sow to the flesh, we shall of the flesh reap corruption. Those who live a carnal sensual life, who, instead of employing themselves to the honour of God and the good of others, spend all their thoughts, and care, and time, about the flesh, must expect not other fruit of such a course than corruption. This only results in a mean and short-lived satisfaction at present, and ruin and misery are the results of it.

But on the other hand, those who sow to the Spirit, who under the guidance and influence of the Holy Spirit do live a holy and spiritual life, a life of devotedness to God and of usefulness and servicableness to others, may depend upon it that of the Holy Spirit they shall reap life everlasting. They shall have the truest comfort in their present course, and an eternal life and happiness at the end of it. Verse 9 cautions us not to be weary in well doing. As we should not excuse ourselves from any part of our duty, so neither should we grow weary from it. There is in all of us too great a proneness to this. We are very apt to flag an tire in duty, yea to fall off from it, particularly that part of it to which the apostle has here a special regard, that of doing good to others.

This therefore he would have us carefully to watch and guard against. He gives this very good reason for it, because in due season we shall reap, if we faint not. If we faint not, he assures us that there is a recompense of reward in reserve for all who sincerely employ themselves in well doing; that this reward will certainly be bestowed on us in the proper season. If it doesn't happen in this world, undoubtedly it will in the next, but then that it is upon supposition that we faint not in the way of our duty. If we grow weary of it, and withdraw from our duties, we shall not only miss this reward, but lose the comfort and advantage of what we have already done. If we hold on and hold out in well-doing, though our reward may be delayed, yet it will surely come, and will be so great as to make us an abundant recompense for all our pains and constancy. ***Preseverance in well-doing is our wisdom and interest, as well as our duty, for to this only is the reward promised.***

Lastly, as the title of this section discusses opportunity, verse states," As we have therefore an ***opportunity,*** it is not enough that we be good ourselves, but we must do well to others, if we would approve ourselves to be Christians indeed. The duty here recommended to us is the same that is spoken of in the foregoing verses. As the apostle exhorts us to sincerity and perseverance in it, so here he directs us both as to the objects and rule of it. The objects of this duty are more generally all men. We are not to confine our charity and beneficence within too narrow bounds, as the Jews and judaizing Christians were apt to do, but we should be ready to extend it to all who partake of the same common nature with us, as far as we are capable, and as long as the stand in need of us. But yet, in the exercise of it, we are to have a special regard to the household of faith, or to those who profess the same common faith, and are members of the same body of Christ. Although we are not to exclude others, yet these are to be preferred. The charity of Christians should be extensive charity, but yet therein a particular respect is to be had to good people. God does well to all, but in an especial manner. He is good to his own servants; and we must in doing food be followers of God as dear children.

As the opportunity presented itself, and as God had come back and re-confirmed the words spoken to my son, at that appointed time of his life, I am truly elated about how God has, and is continuously revealing his word to me. Most importantly, knowing when God shares his word with us, it is not only for us, but it is for us to share and teach others, so that they might know him in the fullness of his glory. Thank God for God and his leading my son to call me. I am aware that that discussion wasn't coincidental.

BOY, WAS I WRONG ABOUT EVERYTHING

It has been almost a year, January 26, 2003, since I have last addressed you the reader. Oftentimes we ask ourselves a number of questions that we have no answers for. When I sit back and ask myself, how I got to this point in my life, my answer undoubtedly, has to be found in the way that I reacted to life's situations, in which I encountered. In chapter 3, "A Right Way of Thinking", I discussed how my wrong way of thinking has allowed me to be in situations now, that I wouldn't even want my enemies to be in. I have learned that there is a battle going on, and the mind is the battlefield.

Ephesians 6:12 states, **"For we wrestle not against flesh and blood, but against principalities, against powers, against the rulers of the darkness of this world, against spiritual wickedness in high places"**. This is the scripture that has helped me to understand how I got to this particular place in my life. My way of thinking was and always is being thwarted and planned against by Satan. Satan attempts to defeat us with strategy and deceit, through well-laid plans and deliberate deception. He sold me a bad bill of goods, and I bought it, for example, the way that I felt about my father. I spent so many years listening to him concerning why my father did or didn't do something, instead of thinking about things as God does. It took my going to Kuwait and hearing from God to finally get a since of direction in the area of thinking. My change of thinking has saved my marriage, my relationship with my children, and my family. It is important to note that my situations didn't change, just the way that I think or thought about them.

I have recently returned from having a wilderness experience in Kuwait. I had planned to get away from my family by volunteering to go to Kuwait, but God took what I meant for bad, and allowed it to work out for all our good. He allowed me to see myself, and the irrational thoughts that I was having. If it had not been for the Word of God and a book written by Joyce Meyer entitled "Battlefield of the Mind- Winning the Battle in Your Mind", I wouldn't be willing to be with my family today. I'm not saying that the enemy has stopped attacking my mind, or that I have totally overcome within my own mind. What I am saying, is that it is a daily fight, but we have access and victory through our Lord and Savior Jesus Christ.

As I speak concerning, a right way of thinking, and I look back on the subject, I remember the sermon that I preached in 1995, "A Right Way of Thinking". Even after sharing that sermon, I never understood the significance of how important it is for a person to think according to the mind and will of God. Although I felt that God had told me He was going to show me how to think right within a years time, it actually took me almost eight years to get to the point that I am at now. I have found out that we can look at things positively or negatively. Depending on the route that one takes, determines how you will respond to situations presented to you, regardless of the expected or unexpected outcome. As you continue to experience life, realize this one thing, the way that you think about the situations in life that you may encounter, will produce either life or death, for that situation. Choose to produce and speak life in every situation that is presented to you.

At this very moment, one of my concerns is where do I go from here? Have you found yourself, asking yourself, this very same question at any point of your life? If so, then you can probably sympathize or understand the way that I am feeling. Let me bring you up to speed. I have returned from Kuwait almost two weeks ago. I was sent to Lundstahl, Germany to get my stomach evaluated. I had previously had three operations on my stomach due to an overly active acid reflux. The procedure is known as a Nissen Fundoplication. This procedure involves the wrapping of your stomach around your esophagus, which restricts the amount of gastric acid that is released from your stomach. Following that procedure, a few months later, I volunteered to go to Kuwait to allow myself time away from my family, and to get the needed time to get to know who and where I was in life. I needed to know what God had in store for me.

Although I was being selfish in nature, it was what I needed to get me where I am today. There is a time in life that one must understand where they are in life, in order to understand where one is able to go, or is suppose to be. The Lord afforded me many more opportunities through this deployment, than I had originally expected. Not on did I begin to see myself through some unlikely sources, I desired and demanded a change within myself through self-evaluations. These changes came following group discussions with brothers about everyday life, or even through Promise Keepers or bible study meetings. It didn't matter how the change came, the important thing was that a change came, and that I seized the moment.

When God presents an opportunity for you to better yourself as an individual, don't allow it to pass you by. The key for me was the having a desire to change for myself first, and for the life of my family. I needed a solid foundation in Christ Jesus, and within myself to be productive, or else I find myself as Paul says in I Corinthians 9:26 as one who is running in uncertainly, beating the air, with no success.

Paul let's me know in chapter 9:24-27 that I should know this; **24 Know ye not that they which run in a race run all, but one**

receiveth the prize? So run, that ye may obtain. 25 And every man that striveth for the mastery is temperate in all things. Now they do it to obtain a corruptible crown; but we an incorruptible. 26 I therefore so run, not as uncertainly; so fight I, not as one that beateth the air: 27 But I keep under my body, and bring it unto subjection: lest that by any means, when I have preached to others, I myself should be a castaway.

It all comes down to the way that I think, and how I proceed with my thoughts, which will determine how if I will allow myself to be self-defeating. This is what is known as the power of choice. God has given us to the free will or choice, to accept or reject Him and His Son Jesus Christ, and Their biblical principles (the Word of God) the bible, (basic instructions before living earth), in order to make us successful here on Earth.

I am in an awoken state of mind, not fully understanding why, but yet thankful for another day. My wife speaks to me half awoke, "Did the Lord wake you up?" I replied yes, but I had to use the bathroom. Oftentimes the Lord allows me to get up early in the morning, so that He can talk to me. I really needed to be talked to. On yesterday I came home in a hurry because my son had a basketball game. My wife needed me to be home as close to five o'clock pm as possible. She had dinner ready and everything. My baby boy wanted to stay home and eat dinner with me. It seemed like the perfect scenario, except for the part when sin entered the arena. The spirit of lust came on me like a flood. I had purchased a pornographic tape, when I was in sin; a couple of years ago, and the urge came on me hard to watch it. I couldn't seem to control that urge. Me, a Man of God, being overtaken in a fault, how could this have happened? I thought I had overcome this type of thing, but I had not. Lord, I need you to come in and deliver me from this state of sin. I am in need of the Lord's help, right now. I don't want to be lost in sin. I have preached and taught the Word of God to so many people, but I myself am being attacked and overtaken so easily. The Word of God says that we are drawn away by our own lusts.

As I look to Brother David, in the book of Psalms, in the Word of God for comfort, I notice the sincerity of his prayers. As he prayed, yet will I do so to the Lord? I ask of the Lord, to forgive me for my transgressions against my own body. He has given me a helpmeet;

therefore there is no need to participate in watching sinful acts on my television. I have sinned against God, for He has given me the power to resist evil. I am ashamed and I do ask for forgiveness from my Father, which is in heaven. I pray that He will forgive me of my transgressions against Him and me. I intend on pressing toward the mark of the prize of the high calling of God, which is in Christ Jesus. I never thought that I was above the ability to sin, but I thought that I would be able to resist it better. Jesus died and conquered sin for all. As He is so are we in this present world, so I should have used His strength to overcome that temptation. I am encouraged the more to let this mind be in me, that was also in Christ Jesus. I have to go for now, my youngest son has awaken and asked me to come and sleep with him. Thank God for a repentant heart, and a will to do what He commands me to do.

I thank and praise Jesus, as Roberto would say, for answering my prayers. Not only did He forgive me for my sins, as it is written in the book of St. Luke 11:4, I know that He is able to lead me not into temptation, but He will deliver me from evil. I have awakened up from sleep, only to find myself addressing these issues of life. I ask myself a very important question, "Where do I stand, right now, as far as my soul is concerned?" I feel confident that God has not only forgiven me, but I believe He's also smiling down at me.

I was blessed on yesterday, although I had been up from about 0135 am, and I didn't get home from work until almost 2000 hrs that night. I was really tired, but my work wasn't finished yet, so I thought. I walked into the house to a wife who was preparing my evening meal, children who welcomed me home, and bath water and lit candles in both my bed and bathroom. Tell me that God won't answer prayers, and I'll tell you that you must not know the God that I serve. The Lord has again allowed me to be awakened early this morning. It is now 0559 a.m., and I have been up since about 0230 a.m., but I have been truly blessed by what God has done in my and my families life thus far.

On yesterday, I visited the physical therapist, who examined my neck and back for muscle strength and deformities. He asked me if anyone had discussed the thought of having to realign my neck, because it is about 3 inches to far forward of my shoulders. I will be starting my physical therapy sessions on today: neck traction exercises. This injury was a result of my car accident that occurred in July of last year, by a drunken driver, whose name will remain anonymous. Although I forgive him, and his insurance company, they are still liable for all my injuries, which occurred, as a result of the accident. This is just another trial that my family and I will have to endure together. Well, my family and I have just finished giving God thanks, during our daily morning prayer, for another day. God has yet again richly blessed us to see another day.

Chapter Five

Relationships:
Spiritual, Natural and Otherwise

FIRST NATURAL

My heart yearns as I set and ponder on my wife. I was reading a book entitled, " Finding God", and the author spoke concerning how we have shifted away from finding God towards finding ourselves. The author went on to say, "Fondness for ourselves has become the highest virtue, and self-hatred the greatest sin. I am in no way judging my wife, but I have an inner emotional pain, because I don't feel that we are spiritually connected or on the same page. I sometimes wonder if we are even in the same book. Can two walk together, except they be agreed?

After all that we've been through, I would have thought that there would have been a yearning, or an out right sprint, for us to come together in worship, as a family. I have developed a much-needed relationship with God, and I long and pray that my wife could have that same type relationship. I realize that we are different people, but our walk in Christ Jesus should mirror his example. I oftentimes use an example of how bitter and sweet water cannot come out of the same fountain and the scripture let's know in the book of St Matthew 6:24 that:

24 No man can serve two masters, for either: for either he will hate the one, and love the other; or else he will hold to the one, and despise the other. Ye cannot serve God and mammon.

As husband and wife, we must be on one accord. Although we may have different ideas or callings in life, there will be a fitly joined connection, which should be to the going out and teach all nations, baptizing them in the name of the Father, and of the Son and of the Holy Ghost. We are to teach them to observe all the things that Christ has commanded of us. He will be us always, even to the end of the world. Neither of our callings, or agendas should cause us to move apart as husband and wife that it causes us to forget where ministry starts first, in the home.

I spoke with my wife on today, while on our way on a lunch date, concerning our walk together in Christ. While sharing the importance of our walking right before Christ Jesus, as the head of the family, I had to get her to understand the need of not allowing any and everything go on in our household. God has been too good to us, and He has brought us from a mighty long way. God has saved our marriage and home life through obedience. We now have a love for each other, but prior to our yielding to God, which was not the case. We have learned that the most important love relationship should be the one we have with Jesus. He embodies the definition within himself. He expressed love in the most definite form possible, by giving His Son Jesus to die on the cross for us. In order for our marriage to continue to prosper we have to learn the lessons taught in this next lesson section entitled "A Submissive Relationship

Then Spiritual

So you find yourself, being by yourself, wondering where or if you belong. So what do you do now? You don't have a clue do you? Neither did I, until I finally decided to hear the voice of the Lord. I thought that I understood the meaning of the word relationship, but not only did I not understand the word; I didn't understand the importance of it. There are various types of relationships and reasons for having them. We will allow you to witness, through reading, some of the different relationships that I have encountered while awaiting the true meaning of the word.

Webster's Ninth Collegiate Dictionary defines relationship as: 1: the state of being related or interrelated 2: the relation connecting or binding participants in a relationship: as a: kinship b: a specific instance or type of kinship 3 a: state of affairs existing between those having relations or dealings b: a romantic or passionate attachment. Neither of these definitions is without merit. All of these definitions are needed to ensure that you and I understand what comprises the whole word, relationship and it's relevance to all of us.

Have you ever heard the cliché, knowing is half the battle. Well, I knew that I wanted to be in a relationship, but the question was with whom did I need to be in one with? I had biological family members, but that relationship didn't work. I had girlfriends and fiancé's, those didn't work either, and so I got married, twice. I got it; I'll have a relationship with the brothers and sisters in the gospel. Wrong again, what I was missing was a true relationship with God. I needed to find God for myself. I finally got my chance to know God personally while doing a second rotation in Kuwait. I was trying to get from everything and everybody, but God had a plan for me to receive that in which I needed most, a relationship with Him.

When God shows you yourself, then you need to be able to move through your problems, while you yet find God. Hebrews 11: 6 let's us know that:

6 But without faith it is impossible to please him; for he that cometh to God must believe that he is, and that he is a rewarder of them that diligently seek him.

The key to seeking God, according to the Word of God, tells me that the duty of man is to seek God. Here are a few scriptures that we can share before I get back to the experiences in which I encountered in Kuwait. The scriptures are as follows:

Deuteronomy 4:29 state: but if from thence thou shalt seek the Lord thy God, thou shalt find him, if thou seek him with all thy heart and with all thy soul (2 Chr. 14:4)

Psalms 105.4 Seek the Lord, and his strength: seek his face evermore.

Isaiah 55:6 Seek the Lord while he may be found, call ye upon him while he is near: (Je. 29:13)

Hosea 10:12 Sow to yourselves in righteousness, reap in mercy; break up your fallow ground: for it is time to seek the Lord, till he come and rain righteousness upon you. (Am. 5:4; Zep. 2:3 Mt. 6:33)

Luke. 11:10 For every one that asketh receiveeth; and he that seeketh findeth; and to him that knocketh it shall be opened.

Acts 17:27 That they should seek the Lord, if haply they might feel after him, and find him, though he be not far from every one of us:

One interesting point worth mentioning is the fact that God has his thoughts toward us. God's thoughts towards include, thoughts of peace, and not of evil and he wants give us an expected end, according to the book of Jeremiah 29:11. He continues by letting us know in verses 12-14, what our expected end will be.

12: Then shall ye call upon me, and ye shall go and pray unto me, and I will hearken unto you.

13: And ye shall seek me, and find me, when ye shall search for me with all your heart.

14: And I will be found of you, saith the Lord: and I will turn away your captivity, and I will gather you from all the nations, and from all the place whither I have driven you, saith the Lord; and I will bring you again into the place whence I caused you to be carried away captive.

There are those who say they have encountered God visibly. They have also said the have heard Him speak audibly as well as having felt His touch physically. Such experiences are possible. Both Old and New Testaments are marked by miraculous, life -changing encounters with God (Isaiah 6:1-8). He has shown, through the pages of Scripture, that He is free to revel Himself in any way He chooses. These supernatural encounters, however, were the exception rather than the rule. While prophets like Isaiah, Moses, and Ezekiel had life-changing visions of God; they did not spend the rest of their lives teaching others to have similar experiences. In some ways it would be nice to believe that experiencing God is liken unto a shaft of light, but as a rule, the truth is far less dramatic.

At this particular moment I am seeing the importance of being able to follow after God, and knowing how to walk with Him. The prophet Amos asked the question in chapter 3:3, "Can two walk together, except they be agreed? If I am to walk with God, one thing is immediately clear, according to what I have read, I must go in the same direction as God. God is not going to negotiate with us concerning the direction that he is going in. He does although invites us to go with Him. God's course is clear. He has committed himself to bringing "all things in heaven and on earth together under one head, even Christ" (Ephesians 1:10). If I want to walk with him, I have not option but to join him on that path. After agreeing to join him, it requires that every ambition in my heart become secondary to promoting Christ. Anything that contradicts this purpose must be abandoned.

Those terms are demanding. Following Christ requires something of us, more than rejoicing in our new identity. Sometimes it may feel like we have to give up our only hope for life. It is interesting that the aforementioned paragraph came up, because I just had that type of conversation with my pastor just a couple days ago. One of my plans when I got back to the states, from Kuwait, was to open a halfway house for ex-cons. But to my surprise, I found out the building that I saw and believed that God showed to me, was being build upon. A thought came to my mind, "What are you going to do now?" I then became confused concerning what God had called me to do. I went to church for 0500 a.m. prayer, and afterwards I had a chance to speak with the pastor. To make a long story short, I spoke with him about what I told the Lord I was going to do. I also let him know that I was a bit unsure where I fit in the ministry, and what I am supposed to do. With wisdom, he proceeded with these words, "What did God tell you to do". He reminded me that we sometimes have good ideas, but sometimes that's all they are, good ideas. We have to be led by, and follow the instructions of God. Then and only then will we be in His Holy Will. I must consciously commit myself to purity of purpose, and

I must renew that commitment regularly, especially when the pain in my heart screams for relief.

Speaking of agendas, I have just returned home from a meeting at the church, which pertains to the prison ministry. The church has an established jail/prison ministry in place, but I have been given the vision to establish a follow-up ministry for convicts being released from incarceration. Herein lies the problem, how do I get to work in the area of ministry in which I have been led to work in. I heard answers from two different sources, one indirectly via radio, and the other indirectly through my pastor. A minister stated on the radio, "In order for a person to be truly successful, one must help others become successful".

A few days later, following Morning Prayer, I had a chance to speak to my pastor about some things that were on my heart. One of the things that I spoke to him about was the idea of opening a halfway house for ex-cons. As I continued to share my thoughts with him, I made a statement concerning a situation that I'm encountering. I told the pastor that I was going to be putting some money away for this vision that I had. I also mentioned to the pastor that the building that I felt I was to have, is being worked on as we spoke, and I didn't know what I was going to do until the Lord had blessed me with a different area. I wanted to know where and what I was to do in the ministry. He politely replied," Did you hear what you said, you think, you felt, it sounds like you are uncertain". What did the Lord tell you to do? I was quickly reminded in my Spirit, that the Lord had shown me years ago, that I would be evangelizing with my brother. My question or concern was and is, what do I do until it happens and how long do I have to wait? I feel that I am not being used in the ministry. Pastor Jackson let me know that my idea was a good idea, but that's just what it was, a good idea, and that I need to do what God had told me to do. He let me know that it is all right to have a good idea, but it is more important to follow God's Will for our lives.

It is amazing how things happen in life when it involves us. It seems as if Murphy's Law is in full effect just when you don't want it to be. I spoke above concerning the vision that I believe, without a shadow of a doubt, it was given to me by God. But look what would happen instead, that which I had proposed to upon my return from Kuwait was being done at my church. Although I had shared this vision with the pastor, it seemed as though he hadn't even considered me. I wondered the normal things; why was this happening, and how could this happen, when both God and the pastor knew what I desired to do in this area of ministry. I thought I was on target; there were at least three other people interested in the same cause. But look at the funny part of it all, it seemed as though I was even in the equation. How could this be, when I had shared this vision with the pastor and the brother, for whom the lead or reigns for this ministry would be given? Here I go again, having the zeal, but not the opportunity. To make matters worse, it seems that as if I were liken unto to the lad who had the two fish and the five loaves of bread; I was just another unsung hero, whom nobody knows.

There has been many times in my walk with Christ that I have felt that I have the gift and I have to use it. I told myself, "Hey your heading in the right direction", only to see the door appearing to shut before me. To make matters worse I felt that God would have the doors open for me to walk through it, because I was following a word given to me by a prophet of God. Then I was awakened by reality. Sometimes in life things don't happen the way we think, but we shouldn't lose hope in our vision. The Word of God tells us that without a vision people perish. On two to three occasions it seems as though I was given the same answer; I was to put my vision on hold. Liken unto the young lad who had the two fish and five loaves of bread, there will be times that you may be "the person that nobody knows". It is difficult for me as a person who strives to achieve, and even more so, because I have a strong desire for ministry. My heart aches to see people looked down upon and not given every opportunity to succeed. I have a heart for the down trodden, and for those who society says they don't deserve another opportunity because they fell or did wrong.

When we come to the understanding that God is a Spirit, and they that worship him in spirit and in truth, then we will have the essence of what is needed to follow Him. It is my determination to follow after God, and I must be willing to wait on the move of God. I'm not saying it is going to easy, but I am willing to follow after the vision that God has given to my pastor. I must believe that God will allow my vision to become reality, while helping to support the vision of our pastor. My relationship with God should be one that allows me to be at peace and total dependence, while demonstrating patience during the waiting period, given us. We must learn how to wait on God, and not move in our time. There is a time and a season for all things. What God has for us is for us, so we shouldn't get intimidated or so caught up in our on visions, that we follow those in whom God has put before us.

A SUBMISSIVE RELATIONSHIP

Any husband who is content to be just "one of the boys" in his wife's eyes isn't much of a husband. Neither is a woman much of a wife if she is satisfied t be just "one of the girls." The intimacy of the marriage relationship carries with it a great sense of mutual commitment that will have a bearing on all of the couple's other activities and relationships.

For far greater reasons, the Designer of human personality is also not satisfied to be just "one of the gods" (Exodus 20:1-6). Yahweh, Provider and Deliver of Israel, the God who came to us in Jesus the Messiah, will not accept a place on the shelf alongside Ra, Krishna, Moon, Allah, GM, or CBS. He has always been a jealous, possessive, commanding God. He will not share His honor with anyone else because no one else deserves that honor (Isaiah 48:11).

God is to be feared more than all others. Most of us don't even like to think about things that frighten us. Whether we're talking about public speaking, high places, cramped spaces, dark nights, noises at the door, or creaks in the attic, the very thought can make us jumpy. Yet without fear, life would be very difficult. Even the animal world is endowed with an alarm and escape mechanism that provides the creature some degree of light or flight necessary for survival.

At no time, however, is the emotion of fear more important or more neglected than when it involves our fear of God. To the extent that we know Him, we will also fear Him. Yet it is a fear, when understood, that calms all other fears and drives us to the Lord, not away from Him. It is a fear that teaches us to love, trust, and totally enjoy Him. This fear might be described as the first step to a personal relationship with God. According to Solomon, "The fear of the Lord is the beginning of knowledge" (Proverbs 1:7). In other words, the fear and knowledge of God go hand in hand.

Nothing and no one deserves to be feared more than the Lord; not people, nor governments, disease, death, nor even Satan. Many who don't know God can't understand this. They assume that the Lord is the only one in the universe who doesn't need to be feared because He is too good and too loving to do us any harm. The ironic result is that such persons often end up missing the very love they seek because their lives are full of fear: fear of failure, fear of people, fear of natural disasters, and fear of accident, disease, and death (Deuteronomy 28:58-68).

Those who really know the Lord take Him seriously. They realize that God expects to be listened to when He warns about moral and spiritual failure (Proverb 8:13, 16:6). He alone determines whether anything or anyone else will be allowed to touch or test us (Job 1); and most important, He alone determines where we will spend eternity (St. Matthew 10:28, Revelations 2:10, 20:1-15). Such authority deserves our respect and fear.

Although we reverence God and stand in awe of His great power, at the same time we can have strong confidence (Proverbs 14:26). With David we can say, "I sought the LORD, and He heard me, and delivered me from all my fears" (Psalms 34:4). A couple of verses later David added, "The angel of the Lord is good; blessed is the man who trusts in Him! Oh, fear the LORD, you His saints! There is no want to those who fear Him" (Psalms 34:7-9). That comes from someone who knew his God. It comes from someone who personally experienced that the God who asks for our surrender is a God who wants us to fear Him for our own good (Jeremiah 32:37-39).

God is to be loved, trusted, and obeyed more than all others. Obedience, like fear, is something we tend to resist. Yet, seeing the importance of such obedience is just a matter of perspective. For example, most of us are happy to obey a stranger's directions when in an unknown area. We don't even think of it as obedience. We see it more like accepting help. That's the way we can look at obedience to the Lord. It is a way of accepting His help and His love that we so desperately need. Obedience is a way of showing that we really do know the Lord and that we are growing in our knowledge of how good, loving, and wise He is.

The apostle John wrote:

Now by this we know that we know Him, if we keep His commandments. He who says, "I know Him," and does not His

commandments, is a liar, and the truth is not in him. But whosoever keeps His word, truly the love of God is perfected in him. By this we know that we are in Him. He who says he abides in Him ought himself also to walk as He walked (1 John 2:3-6).

The fear, trust, and obedience involved I knowing the Lord do not leave us the way we were. They make us better because Christ lives within. They change us until this relationship possesses us and dominates us: bringing us heart to heart and face with the God of all goodness and light.

A SHARED RELATIONSHIP

We all come to God one at a time. In a sense we come all alone. It is our personal decision, our choice, whether or not we are willing to enter into a personal relationship with God. No one else makes this decision for us. But it doesn't stop there. Once we come to God, we are joined to Him and born into His family.

Those who love God will love one another. It is impossible to have a personal relationship with God without also having Christ-centered relationships with other people. Christ's love shown on the cross is our example. He showed us that to be close to the Father means to share the Father's love for others (I John 4:7-11). As I get to know the Lord, I will also be confronted with a God who dearly loves those people around me, my family, friends, neighbors, business associates, acquaintances, and even my enemies.

This is the kind of attitude that Paul encouraged I the Christians at Thessalonica. After affirming the reality and evidence of their relationship to God (I Thessalonians 1:1-7), he went on to say:

Concerning brotherly love you have no need that I should write to you, for you yourselves are taught by God to love one another; and indeed you do so toward all the brethren who are in all Macedonia. But we urge you, brethren, that you increase more and more (4:9-10).

We might like to live in isolation, but we can't do it if we're going to grow in our relationship with God. Knowing God doesn't mean just knowing about Him; it means entering into Him, into His thoughts, His heart, His sacrificial love. Apostle Paul wrote, Beloved, let us love one another, for love is of God; and everyone who loves is born of God and knows God. He who does not love does not know God, for God is love (I John 4:7-8).

Those who love God are dependent on one another. In Ephesians 4, Paul made it clear that our vertical relationship with God is accompanied by many horizontal relationships. He pictured each child of God as a member of the body of Christ. Each part has a function. Just as the eye, ear, mouth, and foot make distinct contributions to our physical bodies, so each believer plays a distinct role in the church, the body of Christ. When every part does its share, the whole receives the benefit (see I Corinthians 1 and Romans 12).

Even though we have received a complete salvation in Christ, there is another sense in which we are not complete salvation in Christ; there is another sense in which we are not complete without relating to and serving one another. We need one another just as much as the mouth needs the eye and the eye needs the hand. This is the outworking of our salvation. We might think we are independent spirits who can do just fine on our own, but we will soon discard that idea as we grow in our knowledge of God.

Those who love God will submit to one another. In Ephesians 5:21, Paul said that we are to submit t one another in the fear of God. In the counsel that follows, his words become very specific. He tells us that:

- Wives are to serve their husbands as a means of serving the Lord (5:22).
- Husbands should lovingly surrender their own interests in behalf of their wives as Christ lovingly surrendered His interests in behalf of the church (5:25-28).
- Children are to obey their parents in the Lord (6:1).
- Servants are to be obedient to their masters as a means of serving the Lord (6:5-7).
- Masters are to show consideration for their servants out of deference to the Lord (6:9).

The message comes though clearly. Knowing God and His love (Ephesians 3:14-21) means that we will lovingly and submissively serve others. As we trust God and obediently serve others, we will discover deep within our own souls the righteousness, wisdom, and power of the love of Christ. Obediently channeling God's love to others enables us to begin to experience the meaning of Paul's prayer in Ephesians 3:14-19.

For this reason I bow my knees to the Father of our Lord Jesus Christ, from whom the whole family in heaven and earth is named, that He would grant you, according to the riches of His glory, to be strengthened with might through His Spirit in the inner man, that Christ may dwell in your hearts through faith; that you, being rooted and grounded in love, may be able to comprehend with all the saints what is the width and length and depth and height to know the love of Christ which passes knowledge; that you may filled with all the fullness of God.

A GROWING SPIRITUAL RELATIONSHIP

A spiritual relationship between God and man is of utmost importance. Christ used the actions of some children to illustrate how we are pattern ourselves after. Sometimes growth starts and then stalls. Even though God Himself is committed to bring us to eventual maturity, He often allows us to remain infantile in our attitudes and knowledge of Him.

The Apostle Paul addressed this issue of immaturity and lack of growth when he wrote:

I, brethren, could not speak to you as to spiritual people but as to carnal, as to babes in Christ. I fed you with milk and not with solid food; for until now you were not able to receive it, and even now you are still not able; for you are still carnal. For where there are envy, strife, and divisions among you, are you not carnal and behaving like mere men? (I Corinthians 3:1-3).

Growing to maturity takes equal amounts of diligence and patience. On one hand, we must never be satisfied with the level of our relationship and knowledge of God. If we are, we'll stagnate, sour, and go backward. On the other hand, we must be patient with ourselves and not expect more than God expects of us.

Scripture shows that this maturity doesn't happen overnight. It requires time to time with God, and time in His Word. For that reason Peter wrote, "As newborn babes, desire the pure milk of the word, that you may grow thereby, if indeed you have tasted that the Lord is gracious " (I Peter 2:2-3). James supported the progressive nature of this relationship with God when he wrote, "My brethren, count it all joy when you fall into various trials, knowing that the testing of your faith produces patience. But let patience have its perfect work, that you may be perfect and completed, lacking nothing (1:2-4).

We should not rush this process. We also shouldn't let it cease to exist either. We must continue to feed on the Word of God even as we allow Him to show Himself faithful in the seasons, tests, and troubles of life. Don't expect perfection. We will fail. Be content to be learning and growing. Don't be like the homeowner who planted a garden, only to dig it up 2 weeks later because he didn't have food, which has not yet grown.

Because life offers its changes, and because of the very nature of spiritual life, our relationship wit the Lord will change. It will change because as we go forward we will always find more and more knowledge and experience of God that will stretch us and enlarge our hearts, allowing us to become better people. Our relationship with God can also change for the worse, however, if we begin to cast and rely on past experiences with Him. We must expect change because our relationship with Him is by nature a contested issue. Our adversary, the devil, won't be satisfied until he devours us and we fall into a spiritual coma (Ephesians 6:10-13). That's the realism that we are faced with. Our knowledge and experience are incomplete. It's as if we are looking at the face of God through a clouded glass. But then it will be face to face. In the meantime, we have our orders. We must accept our incompleteness, trust God, and put your hope in His imminent return. We are to love God and His imperfect family with all of our heart. We can't afford to demand perfection of ourselves. Neither should we demand it of others.

The holiness and growth that God is looking for will be seen in our brokenness and humility, not in our spiritual perfection.

It is not only important for us to give ourselves time to grow in the Lord, but also it is also essential that we take time to let Him show Himself absolutely faithful and satisfying to us. But don't expect in this life what He has promised to complete in eternity. We who trust I Christ are people of eternity. There are no time limits on our future. We are not like the professional athlete who has to reach his goals and make his money and a name for himself in just a few short years before he loses his competitive edge.

Having a relationship with God is not a way to get everything we want in life. It is not the key to financial success, good health, and long life. It is, however, the way to find increasing amounts of inner love, joy, peace, patience, kindness, goodness, faithfulness, and self-control (Galatians 5:22-23). It is a means of finding the ultimate relationship, the ultimate purpose, the ultimate mission, the ultimate security and the ultimate hope.

The only thing that remains for us to do is to trust Christ for what we cannot now see or have. We need to believe that what Christ said to His disciples is still true:

Let not your heart be troubled; you believe in God, believe also in Me. In My Father's house are many mansions; if it were not so, I would have told you. I go to prepare a place for you. And if I go and prepare a place for you, I will come again and receive you to Myself; that where I am, there you may be also (John 14:1-3).

This is our hope. We should not expect the Lord to give us everything we crave now. While He has promised to provide for the needs of all who follow Him, He also reserves the right to determine what we need now and what we will be able to enjoy more of if it is deferred until later.

There are those who say they have encountered God visibly, heard Him speak audibly, and felt His touch physically. Such experiences are possible. Both, Old and New Testaments are marked by miraculous, life changing encounters with God (Isaiah 6:1-8); He has shown, through the pages of Scripture that He is free to reveal Himself I any way He chooses. These supernatural encounters, however, were the exception rather than the rule. While prophets like Isaiah, Moses, and Ezekiel had life changing visions of God, they did not spend the rest of their lives teaching others to have similar experiences. In some ways it would be nice to believe that a relationship with God means experiencing the shaft of light pictured on the front of this booklet. But as a rule, the truth is far less dramatic.

To meet God doesn't mean we have to see Him visibly. We don't need to wait for visions or life-changing dreams. We can encounter God with the eyes of our understanding. Because He is an all-powerful, ever-present Spirit, He can reveal Himself to us at a deeper level than our physical senses. The One who made the world is more than able to give insight about Himself to anyone who wants to know the truth in order to do it (John 7:17; Ephesians 1:17-18). He can also withhold light from those who are more interested in avoiding the truth than in finding it.

To hear God doesn't mean we have to hear Him audibly. There are times when we might wish God would break the silence and whisper in our ear. Or maybe we're glad He doesn't. In either case, it's not necessary for him to do so. If we hear only silence, it is our own self-imposed silence.

For those who want to hear, God can be heard speaking constantly through the timeless wisdom of His book. There are through nature (Psalm 19:1-11), He is always talking to us. Or problem usually is not that God is not speaking, but rather that we're not sure we want to hear what He has already said. For that reason, we need to take seriously the words of the author of Hebrews, who wrote, "Therefore, as the Holy Spirit says: "Today, if you will hear His voice, do not harden your hearts as in the rebellion" (3:7-8). Our opportunity to hear Him on every page of the Bible is a privilege that carries a great degree of responsibility.

To be close to God is not a matter of location. It is common to think that we must go to church to meet God. That makes sense. We meet friends at predetermined times and places. Yet, while God does use scheduled services and addresses, He is not limited to them. He promises to meet us in places of the heart. He wants us to make our hearts His home. James recognized this when he said, "Draw near t God and He will draw near to you" (James 4:8). He didn't say anything about where to go. He didn't tell us to find the highest hill in our area, or a quiet church sanctuary. Instead, James told us to humble ourselves before the Lord (4:10). He gave us reason to believe that wherever we seek Him, the Lord will meet with us there.

David was a songwriter, king, and "man after God's own heart, "shows us why this is true. Deeply humbled by the Lord's constant, unavoidable presence (Psalm 139:1-6), he prayed, "Where can I go from Your Spirit? Or where can I flee from your presence? If I ascend into heaven, you are there; if I make my bed in hell, behold, you are there... If I say, "Surely the darkness shall fall on me, even the night shall be light about me; indeed, the darkness shall not hide from you .... When I awake, I am still with You" (Psalm 139:7-8,11-12,18). Nearness to God is not an issue of location. It is a matter of whether we have place in our hearts for Him.

To know God is not a matter of knowing all about Him. That might be the greatest understatement of all. To know God is not to master Him. At best, we can exclaim with the apostle Paul:

"Oh, the depth of the riches both of the wisdom and knowledge of God! How unsearchable are His judgements and His ways past finding out! For who has known the mind of the Lord? Or who has become His counselor?" (Romans 11:33-34).

Given the limitations of life, our minds can barely begin to grasp the meaning of words that describe God -words like eternal, infinite, all-powerful, all knowing, and everywhere-present. Yet, because He has made it possible to know him, we can begin a process of discovery now that will never end.

We can know God because He has come t us, on our terms, to invite us to Himself on His terms. According to eyewitnesses of the New Testament Gospels, God revealed Himself t us in a person who walked on water, controlled the skies, healed withered limbs, restored sight, and stopped bleeding sores. He fed thousands with a small amount of food, drove out demons, raised the dead, loved deeply, and taught wisely. Living a sinless life, He fulfilled Old Testament predictions, claimed t be the promised Messiah, and sacrificed His own life to secure forgiveness of sins for all who would trust Him. It was this person, known ever since as Jesus the Messiah, who said, "He who has seen Me has seen the Father" (John 14:9). So, according to the Bible, not only is it a personal relationship, it is a Christ-centered relationship.

A CHRIST-CENTERED RELATIONSHIP

Mediators often play an important role in helping to resolve family, labor, and legal disputes. When emotions flare, insight is lost, communications stops, and stubbornness sets in. In such instances, an arbitrator can often bring renewed perspective and a plan for resolution. The ultimate mediator is Christ. Nowhere is a personal go-between more needed than in resolving the conflict and estrangement between man and God. Our personal sin has dug out a chasm so deep and wide that it is impossible for any of us to "cross over" to God on our communication that has come between us.

God is in some ways like a parent who watches his runaway son or daughter become hopelessly entangled with the law. As much as the parent would love to wrap his arms around the child and bring him home, he can't. The law has to be satisfied. Justice must be carried out. A debt to society must be paid and a law must be enforced. For such a need, Christ ahs come to mediate peace between ourselves and God (1 Tim.2:5). Words cannot do justice to the importance of the mediating role of Christ. Without His intervention on our behalf, we could not resolve our differences with God (John 14:6). Without the urging of His loving Spirit, we would never want to.

Jesus deserves our unending appreciation, admiration, and affection. When he wiped out our debt to the law by absorbing our punishment, He proved Himself to be a friend without equal. When He rose from the dead to be life and help to all who trust Him, he gave us a basis for undying hope. When He ascended to the Father's right hand to intercede for us and to act as our personal advocate, He assured that he would provide for us what no mere religion or system of belief could ever offer. He has given to us, and to lead us to a personal relationship with His Father.

Christianity is Christ. As W. H. Griffith Thomas points out in a book by that title, this is the real heart of our Christian faith. We have not been called to a system of laws, traditions, and inspirational ideas.

We haven't been called to the church, to a moral cause, or to the golden rule of Christian love. We have not even been called to the Bible. We have been called to Christ, the mediating person of whom the whole Bible speaks.

The apostle Paul understood the necessity of a Christ-centered relationship with God.

In I Corinthians 1:1-9, he made it clear that he was not promoting a system of ideas. He was speaking of a relationship with God based on,

- **Christ whom we serve (v, 1).**
- **Christ who sets Christians apart (v, 2).**
- **Christ on whose name Christians call (v, 2).**
- **Christ who is our Lord (v, 2).**
- **Christ who gives us grace and peace (v, 3).**
- **Christ who brought us the grace of God (v, 4).**
- **Christ who has enriched us in every way (v, 5).**
- **Christ who is confirmed b experience (v, 6).**
- **Christ for whom we eagerly wait (v, 7).**
- **Christ who will keep us to the end (v, 8).**
- **Christ who will have His day (v, 8).**
- **Christ to whom God has joined us (v, 9).**

Paul's obsession was not a system of new thought, an ethic, a teaching, a form of church organization, or a new program. It was the person he had come to know as the one mediator between God and man (I Timothy 2:5). It was the person who had not only died to pay for Paul's sins (I Corinthians 15:3), but also the person who, through His Spirit, was living His life through Paul (Galatians 2:20) and was his very life (Philippians 1:21).

Here's a question that we can ask ourselves, "Are we as Christ centered as Paul?" Do we realize that true Christianity is found in the living person and personality of the resurrected Christ? Have we learned that Jesus Christ is and must be at the heart of a personal relationship with God? Have we realized that no matter where we look, Christ is there? If we look back in Colossians 1:16, we find that He is our Creator. 2 Corinthians 5:10 tell us He's our judge. By looking up, we find that He is our Savior and Lord in Philippians 2:5-11. Looking down, we see Him as our Sustainer, Colossians 1:17. Looking right, in the book of St Matthews 23:8, He is our Teacher. As we look left, to the book of I John 2:1, Christ is our Advocate. Lastly, looking within, we see Christ as our Life, Galatians 2:20.

There is no question that a personal relationship with God must be a Christ Centered relationship. It is Christ and Christ alone who can bring us to God, cleanse us from the constant pollution of the world, and be our ever-present Source of life and help. It is Christ, the living Word, who reveals, defines, and expresses the personality of the Father. It is Christ who should continually be in our thoughts as Lord and Life. It is Christ who by His Spirit, is a constant presence in and with all who have put heir faith in Him, (St Matthew 28:19-20).

Chapter Six

My Son And I

A father and son united through God. Who ever thought that the day would come, when we would be able to see this with our very eyes? Oh, but we have, it happened to Tony and I. What makes this relationship so special, being that I have other sons? It is the Spirit of God, and a willingness to obey the Word of God. I know that the scripture that says, "What God has joined together, let no man put asunder", is speaking on marriages, but I see that my son and I can't allow the enemy to our souls put us asunder. God forever connects him and me. You have to know the story, behind the story, so I'll tell it to you.

I met Tony's mother in September 1994, in Harker Heights, Texas at Zion Temple C.O.G.I.C. She and Tony happened to be sitting somewhere behind me in the sanctuary on my first night of my being there. But on the second night, she happened to be sitting in front of me. She must have been checking me out that night, and she was, because the next time I saw the woman she had written her name on a piece of paper and put it on the pew. I didn't get a chance to get the paper because my son, Tony, had taken the paper a ripped it up. I had one more opportunity to get to know who she was, when she appeared at a single's meeting. She had on an African pride style dress on that fit every curb that her body could offer. I was in trouble; I had to run outside to speak to the Lord. I told the Lord that I didn't come that far, to that church to find myself lusting after a woman so fine and young. She was so beautiful to me, and she had to have known it. She sat down so eloquently next to me, as if she was luring me closer and closer to her. One thing that impressed me with her, besides her fine exterior (face and body), was her confidence in herself and what she wanted in life. She said she was going to be married before the year was up and she was. Remember, this was the month of September; we were married within a ten day period after that.

This leads us to the relationship between a father and son. There was no relationship between him and me. Yes, I knew she had a child, but I didn't marry him, and he wasn't part of the equation, as far as I was concerned. Then the Lord allowed me to have a wake up call, my wife had to PCS to Korea for a year. I had to ask myself a very important question, "How did all this happen?" Here I am with a child that doesn't know me, and I don't know him. The worst part of it all was that he was 1-½ years old. I was in the military, and now I had become a single parent! Man this isn't going to work; somebody needs to help me! Thank God for a ram in the bush: Mamma and Pappa Hall to the rescue. Tony had to go; I failed him for the first time, but it wouldn't be the last.

As I look back on the whole situation concerning my son, I saw myself as a person who was unwilling to take on a responsibility. I was a selfish person, something that we all can identify with, in one-way or the other. I felt that I wasn't Tony's father or his mother, so why should I be responsible for this child. Little did I know that he was the key to my walk with Christ. A few years later, God showed me the connection between my relationship in Him and my responsibility towards for Tony as one in the same. The key was the relationship. I never knew what it meant to have a true relationship until now. God had to teach me about the true meaning of relationships, by first allowing me to live through one. Tony and I would have to experience my spiritual growth pains together, but I had to first get an understanding of what was really going on in his world. There were a few underlying issues that needed to be understood and dealt with.

My son had been diagnosed as having a Bipolar Disorder with Manic Episodes, Oppositional Defiant Disorder and Attention Deficit Hyperactive Disorder. As its name implies, attention-deficit/

hyperactivity disorder (ADHD) is characterized by two distinct sets of symptoms: inattention and hyperactivity-impulsivity. Although these problems usually occur together, one may be present without the other to qualify for a diagnosis (DSM-IV). Inattention or attention deficit may not become apparent until a child enters the challenging environment of elementary school. Such children then have difficulty paying attention to details and are easily distracted by other events that are occurring at the same time; they find it difficult and unpleasant to finish their schoolwork. They put off anything that requires a sustained mental effort. They are prone to make careless mistakes, and are disorganized, losing their schoolbooks and assignments. They appear not to listen when spoken to and often fail to follow through on tasks.

The symptoms of hyperactivity may be apparent in very young preschoolers and is nearly always present before the age of 7. Such symptoms include fidgeting, squirming around when seated, and having to get up frequently to walk or run around. Tony seemed to have difficulty playing quietly, and he talked excessively. He often behaved in an inappropriate and uninhibited way, blurting out answers in class before the teacher's questions has been completed, not waiting for his turn, and interrupting often or intruding on other's conversation or games.

What I didn't know was that these symptoms occur from time to time in normal children. However, in children with ADHD they occur very frequently and in several settings, at home and at school, or when visiting with friends, and they interfere with the child's functioning. Children suffering from ADHD may perform poorly at school. They may be unpopular with their peers unusual or a nuisance and their behavior can present significant challenges for parents, leading some to be overly harsh.

Again, I found out that the Word of God is true. Hosea 4:6 reminds us that His people are destroyed for the lack of knowledge. Because we have rejected knowledge, He will also reject us. The Word goes on to say that there shall be no priest to him seeing we have forgotten the law of our God, and he will also forget our children. Yes I realize that God was speaking concerning spiritual knowledge, but this can be seen or understood in a natural sense. This demonstrates why it is important that we realize in all our getting we should get an understanding.

But for our relationship, this was only part of the equation that needed to be solved. One has to realize that the weapons of warfare are not carnal, so this fight needs to be fought on a spiritual level, by using the Word of God, against the works of Satan. I learned that the fight was not with Tony and I; it will always be against Satan, regardless of whom I am dealing with.

Prior to leaving for Kuwait, in 2002, while verbally disciplining Tony, something interesting begun to happen. Whatever I said to Tony, the Lord seemed to say to me. I was telling Tony that he was hardheaded, and the Lord allowed me to know that so was I. I continued to let him know that I was trying to teach him the right things to do. Again the Lord repeated the same words to me in my spirit. Although I kept speaking to Tony for some period of time, varying in different topics, the Lord seemed to say the same identical things to me. I didn't understand why the Lord would be saying these things to me. You see, I had given my life to Christ, and I felt that I was heading in the right direction; so I thought. The Lord allowed me to recognize the fact that I hadn't arrived yet. The Lord allowed me to deploy to Kuwait, but that wasn't the end of my lessons concerning relationships. I needed to first learn the true Godly meaning of relationship, and it took me going all the way to Kuwait to learn this. Another obstacle that has to be looked at is the reality of spiritual curses on our families. I had to come to the realization that there are generational curses within my family that need to broken in order for my family to be successful. There will be examples of curses described in chapter seven- "The Reality of Curses".

Chapter Seven

Fighting Against Curses Within
The Family-Through Spiritual Warfare

There are a lot of people, some Christians, some not, who attend church regularly and they try hard to lead godly lives. However, in spite of their best efforts, everything seems to go haywire. Even with their best efforts, nothing seems to help them meet the goal that they set for themselves. Here's an example of what you yourself might have said in the past' "I remember when I use to have this and that, but then I gave my life to Jesus. Now look at what I'm going through. I would have been better off, doing what I was doing." That sounds about as foolish, as Job's wife did, when she told to just curse the Lord and die.

I, as a Child of God, sometimes fail to understand why, despite everything that I have tried to do for my children, they seem to do the opposite of what I have instructed them to do. Yes, I do train my children in the way that they should go, believing that when they get old they won't depart from it. I don't want my children to turn against God and find themselves into destruction. As a Child of God I accepted the Lord with gladness, and I seemed to grow for a while. Then I found myself no longer being able to keep a close relationship with the Lord. The desire to read, study my Bible or pray seemed to become a hard task. Eventually I gave up interest and fell away. The one thing that I despised about myself was the on-again, off-again walk with the Lord.

I was never able to really establish and maintain a consistent walk with the Lord. I found myself battling year after year with all sorts of illnesses, accidents, and marital & family problems. No matter how much I prayed, believed, or attended healing services, nothing seemed to change my life. The conflicts seemed to continue without resolution. It took a devastating toll on my family and myself.

My biological family seemed to be plagued with conditions such as mental illness, alcoholism, physical illness, divorce, incest, poverty, and domestic abuses. Even though some of us came to the Lord, the conflicts appeared to be insurmountable, with no hopes of victory in sight.

Many of us don't realize that the curses, which are in other people's lives can affect us too. Here's an example: If a Child of God continues not to pay his or her tithes and they are a member of the congregation, at a particular church, then the curse is brought into the church. The Word of God let's us know that if we rob God, we are cursed with a curse. It goes on to say even this whole nation. The curse of hindrances is placed in the church. When everyone obeys the Word of God by paying tithes then the church can continue at the pace that God intended. But when we fail to do so then we bring a curse upon the ministry and ourselves as long as we are a part of that ministry.

The problem with curses is again, the effect it has on churches as well as in our individual lives. Many of members, more than ever, are considering divorce and or separation, which are destroying the fabric of our churches, the family. A house divided against itself cannot stand.

Have you ever wondered why people struggle for years, but never prosper or grow spiritually? Why do some churches not grow in spiritual depth or increase in membership? They frequently split up and some members find themselves branching off to start their on ministries. Even when they do seem to have revivals and start to grow, things seem to fall apart; people leave the church, leaving the church where it started off in the beginning. Why do these types of situations occur in the building, that we call the church? These things are the results of curses.

Even though we have been aware of the existence of curses, because of having had them in our lives, we never grasp the full concept of the problem. We haven't begun to understand fully how widespread this problem is in the body of Christ. When we realize that curses are real, and they exist, then and only then can we exercise II Corinthians 10:4-6:

4 (For the weapons of our warfare are not carnal, but mighty through God to the pulling down of strong holds;) 5 Casting down imaginations, and every high thing that exalteth itself against the knowledge of God, and bringing into captivity every thought to the obedience of Christ. 6 And having in readiness to revenge all disobedience, when your obedience is fulfilled.

The purpose of this chapter will be to help you; the readers recognize the hidden battle in our lives so that we can have total victory through our Lord Jesus Christ. In order to accomplish this task, we must first understand exactly what a curse is. The word *curse* is defined as;

Curse - 1: a prayer or invocation for harm or injury to come upon one: imprecation 2: something that is cursed or accursed 3: evil or misfortune that comes as if in response to imprecation or as retribution 4: a cause of great harm or misfortune: torment 5: menstruation

Curse- v to use profanely insolent language against, blaspheme; to call upon divine or supernatural power to send injury upon; to execrate in fervent and often profane terms; to bring great evil upon, afflict

When a curse is placed on someone, the purpose is to cause injury and destruction; sometimes to the point of death. The scriptures of the Old Testament are full of references to curses. The New Testament tells us that Jesus Christ came and died on the cross, conquering Satan, so that we can be set free from curses: Galatians 3:13. Jesus gave His servants the power in His name to break curses.

So we have heard the word curse before, but we're still unsure or ignorant towards the true meaning of the word; so what's it to us. It's everything. Because we are ignorant to the meaning of the word curse, we Christians find ourselves in a defeated state. We can't fight a battle that we don't know about, or we don't even know exists. If you don't know the enemy or his tactics, then how do you expect to pull down the strong holds that he has over you or your family members. Hosea 4:6 states:

6 My people are destroyed for lack of knowledge.

Here are a few more scriptures that speak of the consequences of being ignorant to things that have a great impact on our lives as Christians:

Isaiah 5:13-14
Therefore my people have gone into captivity, because they have no knowledge; their honorable men are famished, and their multitude dried up with thirst. 14 Therefore Sheol has enlarged itself and opened its mouth beyond measure.

Ecclesiastes 7:12
For wisdom is a defense as money is a defense, But the excellence of knowledge is that wisdom gives life to those who have it.

II Corinthians 2:11
Lest Satan should take advantage of us; for we are not ignorant of his devices.

Even with all these scriptures, we first have to come to an understanding that curses are a reality. I have enough since to recognize that curses are still applicable today. I look at my family, and see the curse of alcoholism, drug addiction, bad tempers, poverty, broken homes, selfishness, to name just a few, have overtaken my family. Let's look at what the word of God says about curses happening even today:

Dueteronomy 28:45-46
"All these curses shall come upon you, pursuing and overtaking you until you are destroyed, because you did not obey the Lord your God, by observing the commandments and the decrees that he commanded you. They shall be among you and your descendants as a sign and a portent forever."

Briefly I want to set the stage for the saints, which will lead to the taking us back to the introduction of the book. The introduction covers the topic of obedience leading to deliverance. When you don't fulfill the commandments of God, to include the giving of tithes and offering, you set yourself up for being cursed with a curse.

A majority of believers have a working knowledge of how the sins of Adam and Eve in the Garden of Eden brought about a curse upon humanity and the world I, which they lived. The Lord pronounced specific curses that were related to the serpent, the woman and the man. The curses go a little something like this: The serpent would crawl upon his belly and enmity would be placed between him and the woman and between his offspring and hers (Genesis 3:14-15). The woman would have pain in childbirth and was placed under the authority of her husband (Genesis 3:16). The man who represented humanity was cut off from the tree of life, and the ground was cursed with thorns and thistles so that man would have to toil with great difficulty to produce crops until he died (Genesis 3:17-19). The results of it all were that the man and the woman were driven out of the Garden of Eden and God had the entrance guarded by cherubim and a flaming sword. (Genesis 3:24).

Because Adam and Eve's lives changed, they could not continue to have the comfort they had while they were in the presence of the Lord. They found themselves having blessings being lost, their severe abilities being taken, domain and authority reduced, quality of life changed and their future posterity was also affected. In short, they were in spiritual bondage.

Here's a bit of good news, each of us have a choice between a blessing and curse. Here's the proof found in the word of God.

Deuteronomy 11:26-28
"See, I am setting before you today a blessing and a curse-the blessing if you obey the commands of the Lord your God that I am giving today; the curse if you disobey the commands of the Lord your God and turn from the way that I command you.

Deuteronomy 30: 19-20
"This day I call heaven and earth as witnesses against you that I have set before you life and death, blessings and curses. Now choose life, so that you and your children may live and that you may love the Lord your God, listen to his voice, and hold fast to him."

Because we have a choice to make between a blessing and curse, we must also choose to break the curse. If curses were put into place through sin, then, true repentance must be the starting point if they are to be broken. Only then can spiritual authority be exercised effectively to remove the effects of curses. I had spoken to my mother and a few other people concerning my asking God to allow me to inherit my families' generational curses. To some it may seem to be a prayer that God would not dare to answer, but to me it is one of hope. Because the Lord has allowed me to leave for Him, I want to stand in the gap on behalf of my biological family. I stand not on my own laurels, but on my faith in God. Let's look briefly at some scriptures that deal with curses, as a result of not tithing, and those scriptures that illustrate the power of repentance.

Tithing is a biblical principle from God. Many of us ask ourselves the five w questions, who instituted this system, what is all about, when was it established, where can we find evidence to substantiate paying or not paying tithes, and why is it necessary for us to pay. The most important element of understanding for us knows that the tithes belong to God. The important key to success is the applying of this principle to your life to obtain the promises of God in your life, and rid yourself of the curses on you and those that you love through being obedient to God.

Tithing principles can be found starting with Abram and Melchizedek, the King of Salem, later called Jerusalem; Genesis 14:18-20. Scriptural backing can be found in the following passages: Leviticus 27:31, Numbers 18:24,26,28, Deuteronomy 12:6, 11, 26:12, II Chronicles 31:12, Nehemiah 10:28, 37-38, 12:44, 13:5, Amos 4:4, Malachi 3:8, 10, Luke 18:12, Hebrews 7:5-9. All these scriptures demonstrate a command from God.

As a person who has had some experiences with serving God, more or less not following Him, I have read Malachi 3:8-12 so many times that I can tell you what the scripture says about paying tithes, but I couldn't tell you how true and meaningful it really is until I fell in a place of despair and life filled full of curses. My only hope was to be obedient to the commandment of God. It took my going to Mt Zion Missionary Baptist Church, Hinesville, Georgia, to drop my children off to daycare, and later running into my Pastor and friend (M L. Jackson) to hear a word from God, and for me to get, "A Curse Removed Through the Biblical Principles of Tithing". This wasn't a new word from God, or a newly taught principle from Pastor Jackson. I have heard these scriptures discussed for over 20-25 years, but it wasn't until the 29th day of August 2001, that I received an understanding of the promises of God according to the scriptures. Because of this principle, my relationship with my son Tony, my marriage, and family relationship has had the best opportunity for success. Generational curses will be lifted from the lives of those who choose to be obedient.

Malachi 3:8-12 reads " Will a man rob God? Yet ye have robbed me. But ye say, wherein have we robbed thee? In tithes and offerings. 9 Ye are cursed with a curse: for ye have robbed me, even this whole nation. 10 Bring ye all the tithes into the storehouse, that there may be meat in mine house, and prove me now herewith, saith the Lord of hosts, if I will not open you the windows of heave, and pour you out a blessing, that there shall not be room enough to receive it 11 And I will rebuke the devourer for your sakes, and he shall not destroy the fruits of your ground; neither shall your vine cast her fruit before the time in the field, saith the Lord of hosts. 12 And all nations shall call you blessed: for ye shall be a delightsome land, saith the Lord of hosts".

These scriptures present a promised curse for the disobedience and a blessing for obedience to the Word of God concerning the giving of tithes and offerings. As my life story is depicted in this book you should be able to see how obedience to God through the biblical principle of tithing has both affected my life and those involved with me throughout my life. I'm have come to understand that all things work together for them that love God and are called according to his purpose, Romans 8:28. So everything that I have gone through is for a reason, and now I am able to share this testimony with you the reader and fellow believers in Word of our Lord and Savior Jesus Christ.

Leviticus 26:39-42

"Those of you who are left will waste away in the lands of their enemies because of their sins: also because of their fathers' sins they will waste away. But if they will confess their sins and tier hostility toward me, which made me hostile toward them so that I sent them into the lands of their enemies-then when their uncircumcised hearts are humbled and they pay for their sin, I will remember my covenant with Jacob and my covenant with Isaac and my covenant with Abraham, and I will remember the land."

Jeremiah 14:10,21

"O Lord, we acknowledge our wickedness and the guilt of our fathers; we have sinned against you...Remember your covenant with us and do not break it."

Nehemiah 1:6,7

"I confess the sins we Israelites including myself and my father's house have committed against you."

Daniel 9:8

"O lord, we and our kings, our princes and our fathers are covered with shame because we have sinned against you."

Psalm 106:6,7,13-15

"Both we and our ancestors have sinned; we have committed iniquity, have done wickedly. Our ancestors, when they were in Egypt, did not consider your wonderful works; they did not remember the abundance of your steadfast love, but rebelled against the most High at the Red Sea. But they soon forgot his works; they did not wait for his counsel. But they had a wanton craving in the wilderness, and put God to the test in the desert; he gave them what they asked, but sent a wasting disease among them."

One thing that we must understand is, even though we confess sin, it doesn't guarantee that there is heart felt repentance. When we truly repent through confession, then will repentance of sin become effective. The key to broken curses can be found in II Corinthians 7:10-11:

10 Godly sorrow brings repentance that leads to salvation and leaves no regret, but worldly sorrow brings death. 11 See what this godly sorrow has produced in you: what earnestness, what eagerness to clear yourselves, what indignation, what alarm, what longing, what concern, what readiness to see justice done.

Only until I was godly sorry for my sins against God, was I then made free. I no longer had to try to rationalize and justify my feelings within myself, in order to hide my sins from myself. As Shakespeare once said, "To thine own self be true". With the help of God, I no longer will sin and remain in bondage to sin. I won't be left with an empty self-justified feeling on the inside. I have become responsible for all my actions, and I am leaning on the Lord as my source of strength.

Here's a part B for all concerned as Believers' in the gospel of Christ. Question, does a believer need to fear curses? First of all, the believer needs to realize that we live in a cursed world. There are many people that we will be involved with in our everyday lives. Many of those persons will be cursed, but God has made a provision for us, his people. We should be tuning in on our God who is our source of strength, provisions and protector and not fear the enemy. We as believers should be in agreement with the apostle Paul who said,

Romans 8:31,32
"If God is for us, who can be against us? He who did not spare his own Son, but gave him up for us all; how will he not also, along with him, graciously give us all things?

Romans 8:35-39
"Who shall separate us form the love of Christ? Shall trouble or hardship or persecution or famine or nakedness or danger or sword? As it is written: 'For your sake we face death all day long; we are considered as sheep to be slaughtered.' No, in all these things

we are more than conquerors through him who loved us. For I am convinced that neither death nor life, neither angels nor demons, neither the present nor the future, nor any powers, neither height nor depth, nor anything else in all creation, will be able to separate us from the love of God that is in Christ Jesus our Lord."

We must understand that fearing Satan, his hosts or curses only gives the enemy more power in your life. Fear is not trusting God. It is yielding to the lies and intimidations of the enemy. If the truth will set people free (John 8:32), then believing the enemy's lies keeps people in bondage. God's children must live by the truth.

Secondly, God is able to protect his people from curses. When Balak, the king of Moab called upon Balaam to curse the Israelites, God stopped Balaam from doing it.

"But God said to Balaam, "Do not go with them. You must not put a curse on those people, because they are blessed." (Numbers 22:12)
"However, the Lord your God would not listen to Balaam but turned the curse into a blessing for you, because the Lord your God loves you." (Deuteronomy 23:5)

Thirdly, God has promised protection to the righteous from curses resting on them.

"Like a fluttering sparrow or a darting swallow, an undeserved curse does not come to rest." (Proverbs 26:2)

We must learn to stand on truth and the armor of God will be firmly in place upon our lives. (Ephesians 6:10-18). Also remember, we are fighting a spiritual battle, with spiritual ammunition; the word of God.

Chapter Eight

All That Is In The Flesh

FOR ALL THAT IS IN THE WORLD, THE LUST OF THE FLESH, AND THE LUST OF THE EYES, AND THE PRIDE OF LIFE, IS NOT OF THE FATHER IS NOT IN HIM

First giving honor to God for seeing another day. I thank God for the entire book, but I particularly want to thank Him for this chapter. If we as a people are able to grasp this concept, then we can be successful in God. There are many things in life that cause us to succeed or fail. We need to be fully aware of who we are and what assets are available to us good and bad. This chapter will deal solely with understanding how our stinking, sinful fleshly desires will cause us to end up in Sheol (hell) if we don't totally depend on the Spirit of God to lead and guide us. The word flesh spelled backwards allows you to see the enemy to our soul; (H= his/her) SELF. Our flesh concerns itself only with itself and not the will of God.

What makes a person, who is blessed and highly favored of God; turn his or herself from the presence of God? The flesh will do that very thing. Let's take a moment just to look at the title of this chapter which is comprised of part of I John 2:16. The word *all* is defined as:

All - 1. The total entity or extent of 2. The whole number, amount, or quantity of 3. The utmost possible of 4. Every 5. Any whatsoever 6. Nothing but: only 7. everything taken into account.

So let's take a look at the total entity or extent of the flesh according to Colossians 3:5-9:

5 Mortify therefore your members which are upon the earth; fornication, uncleanness, inordinate affection, evil concupiscence, and covetousness, which is idolatry:

6 For which things' sake the wrath of God cometh on the children of disobedience:

7 In the which ye also walked some time, when ye lived in them.

8 But now ye also put off all these; anger, wrath, malice, blasphemy, filthy communication out of your mouth.

9 Lie not to one another, seeing that ye have put off the old man with his deeds;

This scripture starts off by telling me that there is something inside of us that has to be killed spiritually. Our flesh has to experience shame, humiliation and we have a need to wound its' pride. We need to discipline our flesh to a point that it recognizes, that it doesn't have a choice except follow the ordinances of God. We have to control our body's physical and emotional appetites. Every part of our entity, anything whatsoever must be taken into account when it comes to mortifying our bodies. We must take into account all the things that are in the minds and hearts of men.

Inordinate Affection and Evil Concupiscence

When we read the bible we will find in the book of Exodus 20:12 the 10 Commandments which allows us to know in verse 17, that we should not do these things:

Thou shalt not covet thy neighbour's house, thou shalt not covet thy neighbour's wife, nor his manservant, nor his maidservant,

nor his ox, nor his ass, nor anything that is thy neighbour's" (Ex. 20:17).

That which is here prohibited is concupiscence or an unlawful lusting after what is another man's. In our exposition of the previous Commandments we have pointed out that while their actual terms are confined to the forbidding of outward acts, yet the scope of each one takes in and reaches to the condemnation of everything, which has any tendency or occasion to lead to the overt crime. Here in the final precept of the Decalogue we find clear confirmation of the same, for in it God expressly imposes a law upon our spirits, forbidding us to so much as lust after whatever He has forbidden us to perpetrate. The best way to keep men from committing sin in act is to keep them from desiring it in heart. Thus while the authority of each of the first nine Commandments reaches to the mind and the most secret intents of the soul, yet the Lord saw fit to plainly and literally state this in the tenth, where He specifically reprehends the first motions of our hearts toward any object He has fenced, and therefore it is the bond which strengthens the whole.

Evil concupiscence consists of those secret and internal sins that go before the consent of the will and that are the seeds of all evil. Concupiscence or lusting is the firstborn of indwelling depravity, the first risings and expressions of our corrupt nature. It is a violent propensity and inclination toward what is evil, toward that which is contrary to the holy will and command of God. The soul of man is an operative and vigorous creature, ever putting forth activities suitable to its nature. Before the Fall, the soul of man was drawn forth to God as its supreme Object and the End of all its exercise, but when man abandoned and turned from God as his only Good or satisfying Portion, his soul became captivated with the creature. Thus the soul of fallen man, being destitute of Divine grace and spiritual life, craves sinful objects to the slighting of God, and inordinately lusts after things which in themselves are harmless, but become evil because he neither receives them as from God nor uses them for His glory. Concupiscence, then, is that irregular disposition of soul that is here termed "covetousness."

A further degree of this concupiscence is reached when these evil motions of our corrupt nature are entertained in the mind with some degree of complacency. When a sinful object presents itself before a carnal heart there is an inward response that affects that heart with delight and begets sympathy between it and the object. As in an instance of natural sympathy a man is often pleased with an object before he knows the reason is, so in an instance of sinful sympathy or response the heart is taken with the why he object before it has time to consider what there is in that object which so moves and affects it. At the very first sight of a person we many times find that we are more drawn to him than to a whole crowd of others, though all may be equally unknown to us. So the very first glimpse of a sinful thought in our minds reveals that there is that in us who works a regard for the same before we have leisure to examine why it is so. This second form or degree of concupiscence is harder to eject than the former.

If such evil motions are entertained by us, then an assent and an approbation to sin follow in ones practical judgment, which, being blinded and carried away by the strength of corrupt and carnal affections, commends the sin to the executive faculty. The understanding is the tier of every deliberate action so that nothing passes into action, which has not first passed trial there. Whether this or that action is to be done is the great question canvassed in this court, and all the faculties of the soul await what definite sentence will be here pronounced and thus carried out. Normally two witnesses appear and put in their plea to the understanding or judgment about sin: God's Law and God's vicegerent the conscience. The Law condemns and the conscience cites the Law. But then the affections step in and bribe the judge with promises of pleasure or profit, thereby corrupting the judgment to give its vote and assent to sin. Note how all of this receives illustration in the colloquy between Eve and the Serpent before she partook of the forbidden fruit.

When any sinful motion has thus secured an allowance from the judgment, then it betakes itself to the will for a decree. The understanding having approved it, the will must now resolve to commit it; and then the sin is fully formed within and lacks nothing but opportunity to bring it forth into open action.

"But every man is tempted when he is drawn away of his own lust, and enticed; then when lust hath conceived, it bringeth forth

(open) sin; and sin, when it is finished, bringeth forth death" (James 1:14, 15).

Thus we have endeavored to show what concupiscence or coveting is, and the several degrees of it: the first bubbling up of evil thoughts in our hearts; our delighting in the same (and it is altogether against corrupt nature not to love these firstborn of our own souls); the assent and allowance of our judgment; and the resolution of our wills. Each of these is expressly forbidden by the tenth commandment. And if the sin proceeds any further, then it exceeds the bounds of this commandment and falls under the prohibition of some of the former ones, which more specifically forbid the outward acts of sin.

This final precept, then, utters its solemn protest against sin in the inner life. Herein we may behold and adore the boundless dominion or sovereignty of the great God. He proclaims His rights over the hidden realm of desires. His authority reaches to the soul and conscience and lays an obligation upon our very thoughts and imaginations, which no human laws can do. It would be vain for men to impose statutes upon that of which they can take no cognizance, and therefore our desires and lusting are free from their censure, except so far as they discover themselves by overt acts. But though they escape the commands and notice of men, yet they escape not the scrutiny and sentence of God, for He sees not as men see, neither judges He as men judge. The secrets of all hearts are open and naked before His eyes; not the least breath of a desire can stir in our souls but it is more distinctly visible to Him than the shining of the midday sun is to us.

God's Law, like His knowledge, reaches into the most secret recesses of your soul, searches every corner of your heart, judges those lusts which no human eye can espy, and if they be harbored and approved of, condemns you as a guilty transgressor and worthy of eternal death, no matter how pleasing your external deportment may be. Then how vain it is for us to content ourselves with an outward conformity to God's Law! How we should labor to approve our hearts in sincerity and purity before God; otherwise we are but pharisaical hypocrites who wash merely the outside of the cup while within we are still full of unclean lusts. How many there are who suppose that God's Law reaches only to the outward man, and that, though they entertain and cherish wicked desires and evil purposes in their hearts, so long as these lusts break not forth into external crimes they will not be charged to their account. But the Day of Judgment will show it is far otherwise. How very few reflect upon heart sins! How very few pray, "Cleanse Thou me from secret faults"! Be not deceived, God is not mocked, and He cannot be duped by external shows.

See here the wisdom of God in setting this commandment at the close of the Decalogue, for it is a fence and guard to all the rest. It is from inward defilements of the soul that all our visible sins of word and deed have their rise. All Sabbath-breaking proceeds from the restlessness which is born of unholy desire. "Out of the heart proceed evil thoughts, murders, adulteries" etc. (Matthew 15:19). Observe well that Christ places "evil thoughts" in the front, as the leader of this vile regiment! "Thou shalt not covet." Thou shalt not set thine heart upon, or have the least hankering after, what belongs to another. An objector may say, "It is impossible to prevent the desire for what we admire." Very true, yet in that fact is revealed the fallen condition of man and the desperate wickedness of his heart. That such desire is sinful and damning is only discovered in the light of this commandment. He who honestly faces this final precept in the Decalogue must be convicted of his sinfulness and brought to realize his helplessness, or this is its ultimate design. God has given His Holy Law to us in order that we might see the utter hopelessness of our case if we are left to ourselves. This He has done in order to shut us up to Christ and the magnitude of His grace toward repentant sinners who will believe on His beloved Son, Who perfectly obeyed the Law and in whom the Father is well pleased!

Anger

At some point and time in life we have experienced anger in one form or another. If it wasn't you that displayed this temperament, then possibly, it was someone you now. The word itself gives off a negative aromatic mental smell to it. When you have a moment of anger, you find yourself not being in control of yourself. You have a strong feeling of displeasure and usually of antagonism. The Word of God allows room for anger, but one has to be careful that your anger doesn't turn to rage. Rage suggests that a person has lost their self-control from violence of emotion, often resulting in screaming with in rage. The former state of mind then leads to fury. Fury is the overmastering destructive rage verging on madness. Then there is the infamous indignation that stresses righteous anger at what one considers unfair, mean, or shameful. The worst of them all is wrath. Wrath is likely to suggest a desire or intent to get revenge or a need to administer your own form of punishment. Either way one has to ensure that they do not allow themselves to get to the later stages. Remember you and you alone are responsible for your actions and reactions to whatever befalls you. No one can control you but you.

Malice

Malice leaves you with a desire to see another suffer that may be fixed and unreasonable, or no more than a passing mischievous impulse. The intent may also be to commit an unlawful act or cause without legal justification or excuse. Malice is the twin brother or family member of wrath; both are dangerous and non-Christian like responses.

Blasphemy

The word "blasphemy" is practically confined to speech defamatory of the Divine Majesty. As to the teachings concerning Christ, "blasphemy" against the Holy Spirit, e.g., Matthew 12:32, that anyone, with the evidence of the Lord's power before His eyes, should declare it to be Satanic, exhibited a condition of heart beyond divine illumination and therefore hopeless. Divine forgiveness would be inconsistent with the moral nature of God. As to the Son of Man, in his state of humiliation, there might be misunderstanding, but not so with the Holy Spirit's power demonstrated.

Filthy Communication

The bible warns us against filthy communication being in our members throughout the Word of God. We have a member in our body known as the tongue, which is the primary instrument, used in filthy communication. St James 3:6 reads:

And the tongue is a fire, a world of iniquity: so is the tongue among our members, that it defileth the whole body, and setteth on fire the course of nature; and it is set on fire of hell.

Speak not evil one of another, brethren. He that speaketh evil of his brother, and judgeth his brother, speaketh evil of the law, and judgeth the law: but if thou judge the law, thou art not a doer of the law, but a judge. (St James 4:11)

When we speak using filthy communication we are speaking things that may hurt or injure another. We must not speak evil things of others, though they be true, unless we are called to it, and there be some necessary occasion for it. We should much less report evil things when they are false, or, for aught we know, may be so. The law of kindness, as well as truth and justice must guide our lips. This, which Solomon makes as a necessary part of the character of his virtuous woman; **that she openeth her mouth with wisdom, and in her tongue is the law of kindness (Proverb 31:26).** We should not speak evil of one another. Since Christians are brethren, they should not defile nor defame one another. It is required of us that we be tender of the good name of our brethren. If we don't have anything good to say, we shouldn't speak evil things of each other instead. We shouldn't take pleasure in making known the faults of others, divulging things that are secret, neither merely to expose them, nor to make more of their known faults than they really deserve. We shouldn't make up false stories and spread things concerning them of which they are totally innocent of having committed.

Seeing then, after taking everything into account; there is an enemy warring inside our members to destroy our souls. For all that is in the world are the lust of the flesh, and the lust of the eyes, and the pride of life. We can't afford to use those things, which will cause the wrath of God to come to those, the children of disobedience. We must die to the flesh (H= his/her SELF). We are called to a "Higher Standard of Living".

Chapter Nine

Called to a Higher Standard of Living

A Message to Preachers
A.W. Pink

In this message we purpose to treat of those things which have a particular bearing upon those whom God has called to preach and teach His Word: those whose whole time and energies are to be devoted unto seeking the spiritual and eternal welfare of souls, and the better equipping of themselves for that most blessed, solemn and important work. Their principal tasks are to proclaim God's Truth and to exemplify and commend their message by diligently endeavoring to practice what they preach, and setting before their hearers a personal example of practical godliness. Since it be the Truth they are to preach, no pains must be spared in seeing to it that no error be intermingled therewith, that it is the pure milk of the Word they are giving forth. To preach error instead of Truth is not only grievously to dishonor God and His Word, but will mislead and poison the minds of the hearers or readers.

The preacher's task is both the most honorable and the most solemn of any calling, the most privileged and at the same time the most responsible one. He professes to be a servant of the Lord Jesus Christ, a messenger sent forth by the Most High. To misrepresent his

Master, to preach any other gospel than His, to falsify the message which God has committed to his trust, is to sin of sins which brings down upon him the anathema of heaven, (Gal. 1:8) and will be visited with the sorest punishment awaiting any creature. Scripture is plain that the heaviest measure of divine wrath is reserved for unfaithful preachers (Matt. 23:14; Jude 13). Therefore the warning is given, "be not many masters, knowing that we shall receive the greater condemnation: (James 3:1) if unfaithful to our trust. Every minister of the Gospel will yet have to render a full account of his stewardship unto the One who he claims called him to feed His sheep, (Heb. 13:17), to answer for the souls who were committed to his charge. If he fails to diligently warn the wicked, and he dies in his iniquity, God declares "his blood will I require at thine hand" (Ezek: 3:18).

Thus the chief and constant duty of the preacher is to conform unto that injunction "Study to show thyself approved unto God a workman that needeth not to be ashamed, rightly dividing the word of truth" (2 Timothy 2:15). In the whole Scripture there is no exhortation addressed t preachers which is of greater import than that one, and few equal. Doubtless that is why Satan has been so active in seeking to obscure its first two clauses by raising such a cloud of dust over the last one. The Greek word for "study" here signifies "give diligence": spare no efforts, but make it your paramount concern and constant you're Master. Seek not the smiles and flatteries of worms of the earth, but the approbation of the Lord. That is to take precedence to everything else: unless it is, aims to commending thyself unto God- thine own heart and character, thy dealing with and walk before Him, ordering all thy ways according to His revealed will. What is your "service," your ministrations, worth if He is displeased with thee?

"A workman that needeth not to be ashamed." Be conscientious, diligent, and faithful, in the use you make of your time and the talents God has entrusted to you. Give unremitting heed to that precept, "Whatsoever thy hand findeth to do, do it with thy might" (Eccl. 9:10)- put your very best into it. Be industrious and assiduous, not careless and slovenly. See how well you can do each thing, not how quickly. The Greek word for "workman is also translated "laborer," and in twentieth century, English might well be rendered "toiler."

The ministry is no place for triflers and idlers, but for those who are prepared to spend and be spent in the cause of Christ.

The preacher ought to work harder than the miner, and to spend more hours per week in his study than does the man of business in his office. A workman is the very opposite of a shirker. If the preacher is to show himself approved unto God and be a workman that needeth not to be ashamed, then he will have to labor while others sleep, and do so until he sweats mentally.

"Meditate upon these things; give thyself wholly to them; that thy profiting may appear to all. Take heed unto thyself, and unto the doctrine; continue in them: for in doing this thou shalt both save thyself, and them that hear thee: (1 Tim 4:15, 16). This is another part of the mandate which Christ has laid upon His official servants, and a most comprehending and exacting one it is. He requires them to put their hearts into the work, to give the whole of their thoughts to it, to lay themselves completely out in it, to devote all their time and strength thereto. They are to keep clear of all secular affairs and worldly employments, and to show all diligence in the task assigned them. That it is an arduous task appears from the different designations given them. They are called "soldiers" to denote the exertions and fatigue which attend the proper discharge of their calling; "overseers and watchmen" to intimate the care and concern which accompany their office; "shepherds and teachers" to signify the various duties of leading and feeding those committed to their charge. But first and foremost they are to take heed to their personal growth in grace and piety, if they would minister effectually unto others.

Particularly does the minister need to attend unto this injunction "take heed unto thyself: in his study of the Scriptures, reading them devotionally ere he does so professionally; that is seeking their application and blessing to his own soul before searching for sermonic materials. As the saintly Hervey expressed it, "Thus may we always be affected when we study the Oracles of Truth. Study them not as cold critics, who are only to judge of their meaning, but as persons deeply interested in all they contain. Who are particularly addressed in every exhortation, and directed in every precept. Whose are the promises, and to whom do they belong. When we are enabled thus to promises, and to whom belong the precious privileges.

When we are then enabled thus to realize and appropriate the contents of that invaluable Book, then shall we taste the sweetness and feel the power of the Scriptures. Then shall we know by happy experiences that our Divine Master's words are barely sounds and syllables, but that "they are spirit and they are life." No man can be constantly giving out- that which is fresh and savory- unless he is continually taking in. That which he is to declare unto others is what his own ears have first heard, his own eyes seen; his own hands have handled (1 John 1:1, 2).

The mere quoting of Scripture in the pulpit is not sufficient-people can become familiar with the letter of the Word by reading it at home; it is the expounding and application of it which is so much needed. "And Paul, as his manner was ... reasoned with them out of the Scriptures, opening and alleging that Christ must needs have suffered, and risen from the dead" (Acts 17:2,3). But to "open" the Scripture helpfully to the saints requires something more than a few months' training in a Bible Institute, or a year or two in a seminary. None but those who have been personally taught of God in the hard school of experience are qualified to so "open" the Word that divine light is cast upon the spiritual problems of the believer, for while Scripture interprets experience, experience is often the best interpreter of Scripture. "The heart of the wise teacheth his mouth, and addeth learning to his lips," (Proverbs 16:23), and that learning cannot be acquired in any man's faith by studying certain passages of Scriptures. The one is acquired through painful discoveries of the plague of our hearts, and the other is increased by a deepening acquaintance with God. We must ourselves be comforted of Him before we can comfort others (2 Corinthians 1:4).

"To seek after mere notions of Truth, without an endeavor after an experience of its power in our hearts, is not the way to increase our understanding in spiritual things. He alone is in a posture to learn from God, who sincerely gives up his mind, conscience, and affections to the power and rule of what is revealed unto him. Men may have in their study of the Scriptures other ends also, as the profit and edification of others. But if this conforming of their own souls unto the power of the Word be not fixed in the first place in their minds they do not strive lawfully, nor will they be crowned. And if at any time, when we study the Word, we have not this design expressly in our minds, yet if upon the lost of our principal advantage by it" (John Owen). It is much to be feared that many preachers will have reason to lament in the day to come, "They made me the keeper of the vineyards; but mine own vineyard have I not kept" (Song of Solomon 1:6) - like a chef preparing meals for others and himself starved.

While the preacher is to pander the Word devotionally, he is also to read it studiously. If he is to become able to feed his flock with "the finest of the wheat" (Psalms 81:16) then he must needs study it diligently and daily, and that to the end of his life.... Alas, that so many preachers abandon their habit of study as soon as they are ordained! The Bible is an inexhaustible mine of spiritual treasures, and the more its riches are opened to us (by hard digging) the more we realize how much there is unpossessed, and how little we really understand what has been received. "If any man think that he knoweth anything, he knoweth nothing yet as he ought to know" (1 Corinthians 8:2).

The Word of God cannot be understood without a constant and laborious study, without a careful and prayerful scrutiny of its contents. This is not to say that it is recondite and obscure. No, it is as plain and intelligible as in the nature of things it can be, adopted in the best possible manner to give instructed by the best possible means of instruction who will not take pains with the same. Promise of understanding is not made to the dilatory and indolent, but to the diligent and earnest, to those who seek for spiritual treasure (Proverbs. 2:3, 5). The Scriptures have to be searched, searched daily, persistently and perseveringly, if the minister is to become thoroughly familiar with the whole of what God has revealed, and if he is to set before his hearers "a feast of fat things." Of the wise preacher it is said, "sought to find out acceptable words" (Eccl. 12:9, 19), as if his whole soul was engaged in the discovery of the best mode as well as the best substance of instruction.

No preacher should be content with being anything less than "a man mighty in the Scriptures" (Acts 18:24). But to attain thereunto he must subordinate all other interests. As an old writer quaintly said, "The preacher should be with his time as the miser is with his gold- saving it with care, and spending it with caution." He must also remind himself constantly whose Book it is he is about to take up, so that he ever handles it with the utmost: reverence and can aver: my heart standeth in awe of Thy word: (Psalms 119:161). He must ever come to it in the spirit of prayer, crying "that which I see not teach Thou me" (Job 34:32): the enlightening grace of the Spirit will, often open mysteries to the meek and dependent which remain closed to the most learned and scholarly. A holy heart is equally indispensable for the reception of supernatural truth, for the understanding is clarified by the purifying of the heart. Let there also be a humble expectation of divine help, for "according to your faith be it unto you" holds good here, too.

It is only by giving heed to the things which have been pointed out in the preceding paragraphs that the necessary foundations are laid for any man's becoming a competent expositor. The task before him is to unfold, with clearness and accuracy, the Word of God. His business is entirely exegetical - to bring out the true meaning of each passage he deals with, whether it accords with his own preconception or no. As it is the work of the translator to convey the real sense of the Hebrew and Greek into English, so the interpreter's is to apprehend and communicate the precise ideas which the language of the Bible was meant to impart. As the renowned Bengel so well expressed it, "An expositor should be like the maker of a well who puts not water into it but makes it his object to let the water flow, without diversion, stoppage, or defilement." In other words, he must not take the slightest liberty with the sacred text, nor give it a meaning which it will not legitimately bear; neither modifying its force nor superimposing upon it anything of his own, but seeking to give out its true import.

To comply with what has just been said calls for an unbiased approach, an honest heart and a spirit of fidelity on the part of the interpreter. "Nothing should be elicited form the text but what is yielded by the fair and grammatical explanation of its language" (Patrick Fairbairn). It is easy to assent to that dictum, but often difficult to put into practice. A personal shrinking from what condemns the preacher, a sectarian bias of mind, the desire to please his hearers, have caused not a few to evade the plain force of certain passages, and to foist on them significations which are often quite foreign to their meaning. Said Luther, "We must not make God's Word mean what we wish. We must not bend it, but allow it to bend it, but other than that is highly reprehensible. Great care needs ever to be taken that we do not expound our own mind instead of God's. Nothing can be more blameworthy than for a man to profess to be uttering a "Thus saith the Lord" when he is merely expressing his own thoughts. Yet who is there who has not, unwittingly, done so?

If the druggist is required by law to follow exactly the doctor's prescription, if military officers must transmit the orders of their commanders verbatim or suffer severe penalties, how much more incumbent it is for one dealing with divine and eternal things to adhere strictly to his textbook! The interpreter's task is to emulate those described in Neh. 8:8, of whom it is said, "they read in the book of the law of the Lord God distinctly, and gave the sense, and caused them to understand the reading." The reference is unto those who had returned to Palestine from Babylon. While in captivity they had gradually ceased to use Hebrew as their spoken language, Aramaic displacing it. Hence there was a real need to explain the Hebrew words in which the Law was written (cf Neh. 13:23, 24). Yet the recording of this incident intimates that it is of permanent importance, and has a message for us. In the good providence of God there is little need today for the preacher to explain the Hebrew and the Greek, since we already possess a reliable translation of them into our own mother tongue though occasionally, yet very sparingly, he may do so. But his principal business is to "give the sense" of the English Bible and cause his hearers to "understand" its contents. His responsibility is to adhere strictly to that injunction, "let him speak My word faithfully. What is the chaff to the wheat? Saith the Lord" (Jer. 23:28). - Arthur W. Pink

After reading Arthur W. Pink's, "Message to a Preacher", and thinking back on a conversation with the brethren in Kuwait, I can not only see why Gomer felt the way she did, because I too feel the pain in this poem entitled, "Gomer's Song", written by J. Marcus Weekley.

GOMER'S SONG

I am Gomer*
Lying in my darkness
And you beside me,
My heart again, cold to you
I've turned you away
With my unfaithfulness
Like a piece of glass
In your heart
Or a bad wine,
I am sour on your tongue,
Bitter tears,
My heart breaks and
Still, I turn you away
My body my weapon dark,
Used over, over, over,
Stabbing, stabbing,
Merciless, I hear your breathing
See your chest rise, you in peace,
And wonder
Why am I here?
Why do you?
Still love me?
Why do you still love me?
I cry.

"Therefore his sisters sent unto him, saying, Lord, behold he whom thou lovest is sick."

When Jesus heard that, he said, this sickness is not unto death, but for the glory of God that the Son of God might be glorified thereby.

"And, behold, there was a woman which had a spirit of infirmity eighteen years, and was bowed together, and could in no wise lift up herself.

And when Jesus saw her, he called her to him and said unto her, Woman, thou art loosed from thine inifirmity.

And he laid his hands on her: and immediately she was made straight, and glorified God.

Chapter Ten

This Sickness Is Not Unto Death

We all have unique personal histories. We may have had a relatively uneventful life, while others have endured many hardships. Some of you may have had emotional and physical scars from your past, while others may have had others problems to deal with. I myself have had medical problems from the onset of my birth. This is why it is understandable when men blame the past for their present troubles. However just as God uses your past problems for his glory, I know he can use your current medical conditions to show his glory also. Romans 8:28 reads:

28 And we know that all things work together for good to them that love God, to them who are the called according to his purpose.

Even though the tragedies of life often force us to cry out to God, we need to watch as he takes our situations and brings glory to himself and blessings to us. It would be sad for me to hold bitterness against God and blame him for what I am currently enduring in my body. God loves me dearly and he is bringing me through these trials so that I can experience his deeper presence in my life. God spared me to have a life filled with joy in my salvation and to give me the purpose and meaning for which I may be searching. I had to realize that God is consciously aware of my every need and condition, and He's a Father who loves me.

I don't have to wonder whether or not my past is to sinful for God to show mercy on me. God doesn't take us just the way we are. He takes us in spite of the way we are. He takes our willing heart, regardless of our past, and creates a new heart, one that seeks after God. When that happens to us, we will know it is God who is doing the work.

God can use each life experience to shape a man. He can use our medical conditions as tools to prepare us for ministry to others. God will bring circumstances in our lives to remind us of how he has delivered us, and he will do the same thing for others. We can use our experiences as a source of encouragement for others as we share how God was faithful through our struggles and victories. Each situation that we face in life further builds our character.

Character is not only shaped by crisis; it is reveled in crisis. When crises occur, you can discover more about yourself as you listen to the words that come out of your mouth, as you see what actions you take, and as you monitor your attitude and evaluate how Christ like it is.

Life's circumstances teach us most about our character and God's faithfulness. God can use both our failures and our successes for his glory. He can take what we have done to ourselves and what others have done to us for his glory. Remember, "Where sin abounded, grace abounded much more."

Nothing life brings your way is beyond God's ability to use for his purposes. Ephesians 2:10 declares that we are God's handiwork, born again through Jesus to do all the good things that God has planned for his kingdom. It probably is not hard to think of how God has taken something from someone else's past and used it to do a good work. It might be harder to imagine how our own past can be redeemed by God and used in the future. Moses makes a good case study for God's ability to shape men for his use.

I want to take a moment to explain some of the physical ailments within my own body that the Lord is going to use to show his glory. I believe that God is able to take any situation and make it work for your good. This opportunity will allow me to offer you, the reader, some educational information concerning GERD, a medical condition that I am presently dealing with that affects over 7 million people in the U.S. alone. It may not be you this time, but it may affect someone that you really care about. So get smart and get educated.

Common Questions Concerning GERD

1. What is GERD?

GERD stands for **G**astro**e**sophageal **R**eflux **D**isease. Gastroesophageal reflux describes a backflow of acid from the stomach into the swallowing tube or esophagus. This acid can irritate and sometimes damage the delicate lining on the inside of the esophagus. Almost everyone experiences gastroesophageal reflux at some time. The usual symptom is heartburn, an uncomfortable burning sensation behind the breastbone, most commonly occurring after a meal. In some individuals this reflux is frequent or severe enough to cause more significant problems, that is a disease. Thus, gastroesophageal reflux *disease* is a clinical condition that occurs when reflux of stomach acid into the esophagus is severe enough to impact the patient's life and/or damage the esophagus.

For more information about GERD and an educational multimedia walk-through, refer to the <u>Introduction to GERD</u>.

2. I have never heard of GERD. Is it a new disease?

No. GERD has probably been around as long as heartburn. The term is relatively new (about 20 years), however, and has really come into common usage over the past few years. GERD is often called "reflux," "reflux esophagitis," or sometimes even "<u>hiatus hernia</u>" (although hiatus hernia is a specific diagnosis that may or may not have anything to do with GERD). GERD is the preferred term because it accurately describes the problem - reflux of stomach acid up into the esophagus where it can produce symptoms and sometimes damage. Many patients and health care professionals are not familiar with GERD and its potential consequences, and thus may not have heard the term previously.

3. What are some symptoms of GERD?

The four major symptoms of GERD are:

- Heartburn (uncomfortable, rising, burning sensation behind the breastbone).
- Regurgitation of gastric acid or sour contents into the mouth.
- Difficult and/or painful swallowing.
- Chest pain.

Heartburn is the most common symptom of GERD. In some patients it may be accompanied by other GERD symptoms, such as regurgitation of gastric contents into the mouth, chest pain and difficulty swallowing. Pulmonary manifestations, such as asthma, coughing, or intermittent wheezing and vocal cord inflammation with hoarseness, occur in some GERD patients.

In addition, acid can be regurgitated into the lungs in some GERD patients, causing wheezing or cough. Acid refluxed into the throat can cause sore throat. If acid reaches the mouth, it can dissolve enamel of the teeth.

4. How do people get GERD? What causes GERD?

GERD is caused by reflux of stomach acid into the esophagus. In most patients this is due to a transient relaxation of the "gate" or sphincter that keeps the lower end of the esophagus closed when a person is not swallowing food or liquids. This transient relaxation happens a few times each day in people without GERD. Why it happens more frequently in GERD patients isn't known. The esophagus is not able to cope with acid as well as the stomach and is easily injured. It's the acid refluxing into the esophagus that produces the symptoms and potentially damages the esophagus.

5. How many people are afflicted with GERD?

Recent statistics from the US Department of Health and Human Services indicate that about seven (7) million people in the US alone suffer from GERD.

(Source: Digestive Diseases in the United States: Epidemiology and Impact, National Digestive Diseases Data Working Group, James E. Everhart, MD, MPH, Editor, US Department of Health and Human Services, Public Health Service, National Institutes of Health, NIH Publication No. 94-1447, May 1994)

6. Who is afflicted with GERD?

GERD afflicts people of every socioeconomic class, ethnic group and age. However, the incidence does seem to increase quite dramatically above the age of 40. Greater than 50 percent of those afflicted with GERD are between the ages of 45-64 (both male and female).

7. Do children get GERD?

Yes. GERD is most common in adults over age 40 but virtually anyone can get GERD, even infants.

8. What is the difference between heartburn and GERD?

GERD is a disease and heartburn is its most common symptom. Heartburn is defined as a rising, burning sensation behind the breastbone caused by reflux of stomach acid into the esophagus. Nearly everyone has or will experience heartburn on occasion. Frequent heartburn that disrupts one's lifestyle suggests the diagnosis of GERD.

9. What is the difference between GERD and a hiatus hernia?

Hiatus hernia refers to dislocation of the stomach through the "hiatus" of the diaphragm and into the chest. This is a common condition that increases in frequency with age. It may or may not be associated with GERD. When GERD is severe enough to be complicated by erosive esophagitis, seen as breaks in the lining of the esophagus, a hiatus hernia is usually present. However, most patients with a hiatus hernia do not have GERD.

10. What is endoscopy and when is it used in GERD patients?

Endoscopy is a diagnostic test wherein a thin, flexible tube is swallowed by the patient to allow the physician to directly inspect the lining of the upper gastrointestinal tract. This procedure can be used to identify complications of GERD and to take small samples (biopsies) for further analysis. GERD patients who have certain symptoms, such as difficulty in swallowing or painful swallowing, should be considered for endoscopy. Patients who fail to respond to therapy are also candidates for endoscopy. Some physicians advocate endoscopy for all patients with long-standing GERD in order to rule out Barrett's esophagus.

11. What are the complications of GERD?

Only a minority of patients develop complications of GERD. These complications include breaks in the lining of the esophagus (esophageal erosions), esophageal ulcer, and narrowing of the esophagus (esophageal stricture). In some patients, the normal esophageal lining or epithelium may be replaced with abnormal (Barrett's) epithelium. This condition (<u>Barrett's esophagus</u>) has been linked to cancer of the esophagus and must be carefully watched. Lung (pulmonary) aspiration, asthma and inflammation of the vocal cords or throat may also be caused by GERD.

12. What makes GERD symptoms worse?

The major factor is meals. Meals stimulate the stomach to produce more acid that can reflux up into the esophagus. In some patients, lying down or taking certain medications can worsen acid reflux.

13. Does eating spicy food cause GERD or make GERD worse?

Spicy foods do not cause GERD, although they do seem to worsen GERD symptoms in some people. Food (in general) can make GERD worse. This is because food fills the stomach and induces more transient relaxations of the lower esophageal sphincter. In addition, *all* meals stimulate acid production in the stomach to aid digestion and can increase reflux into the esophagus in GERD sufferers. Any very large meal might be expected to produce heartburn in some people. The spicy food story is so compelling, however, that GERD sufferers often relate a spicy (or greasy) meal to their symptoms. Often they are told to avoid certain foods whether or not these foods have anything to do with their symptoms. In this way, many GERD sufferers end up on a very restricted diet or end up blaming their symptoms on dietary indiscretion. If avoiding spicy foods and/or other dietary advice helps, that's great. If it doesn't, GERD sufferers shouldn't feel that they are doing something wrong. They should seek medical advice on managing their disease.

14. Do any medications make GERD worse?

Yes. Medicines that delay emptying of acid from the stomach or that increase acid backup into the esophagus can worsen GERD. If you have, or suspect you have, GERD and you require medication for other conditions, you should make sure you inform your doctor about all medications you are taking including prescription and over-the-counter medications.

15. What should people with GERD avoid?

GERD is a disease that is caused by gastric acid. However, certain foods can trigger symptoms in some patients. If you lie down after a meal, or wear tight-fitting clothing, and perform certain activities, such as bending over, will cause these symptoms to be triggered in a patient. A good way to identify these "triggers" is to keep a diary of GERD symptoms noting when they occur. If symptoms follow a pattern and occur after certain foods or activities, these foods or activities should be avoided. A diary will also help patients continue to enjoy those foods or activities that do not seem to provoke symptoms, so that their lifestyle is not restricted unnecessarily. Patients should review their symptoms with their doctor, who can evaluate their condition and advise an appropriate treatment plan.

16. Can GERD cause cancer?

Severe, long-standing GERD can damage the esophagus and cause a condition known as <u>Barrett's esophagus</u> wherein the normal lining of the esophagus is replaced by a lining more like that of the stomach or intestine. It is thought that this replacement may be an attempt by the body to protect itself from further injury by acid. The risk of esophageal cancer appears to increase significantly in patients with Barrett's esophagus. The only way to diagnose Barrett's esophagus is by endoscopy. Some studies suggest that intensive treatment of Barrett's esophagus can reduce the amount of abnormal lining in the esophagus. It is not yet clear whether such treatment will prevent esophageal cancer in GERD patients, but this is under active investigation.

17. Are there long-term consequences of GERD?

Long-standing GERD can lead to damage of the esophagus. This damage usually consists of breaks in the lining of the esophagus. In some cases ulcers can develop. In some patients, such damage can result in scarring and narrowing of the esophagus, making swallowing painful or difficult. A condition called <u>Barrett's esophagus</u> is thought to result from long-standing GERD in some patients. Barrett's esophagus is a risk factor for the development of esophageal cancer. In some patients, acid backup caused by GERD is thought to result in damage to the vocal cords or teeth and may even cause asthma.

18. Is there relationship between GERD and asthma?

Many investigators believe that there is a link between asthma and reflux of stomach acid up into the throat and then down into the lungs in some patients. It appears that some patients who suffer from asthma might benefit from treatment of GERD. This is a topic of active research at the moment.

19. Can GERD cause inflammation of the throat?

In some patients, acid can reflux into the throat causing inflammation of the back of the throat which can lead to pharyngitis, or into the vocal cords, which can lead to laryngitis and hoarseness. Although there are many other causes for sore throat and laryngitis, GERD should be suspected in a patient with chronic sore throat or other GERD symptoms or when no other cause can be found.

20. Can GERD be cured?

Unfortunately, GERD, in general, cannot be cured at present. In some cases, it may be a temporary condition associated with a specific aggravating factor such as pregnancy. In such cases, GERD will go away on its own when the pregnancy has ended. In most cases GERD is a chronic condition. However, it can be effectively managed with medications and lifestyle modifications in almost everybody. In severe cases, surgery is an option. Surgery does not cure the underlying problem, but wraps part of the stomach around the lower end of the esophagus to help keep acid from getting back up into the esophagus. A doctor can evaluate the condition and advise you on an appropriate treatment plan.

21. I think I have GERD. What should I do?

See your doctor. Your doctor can establish the diagnosis and work with you to get you symptom-free. Primary care and physicians of many specialties are becoming increasingly familiar with GERD. Gastroenterologists and some gastrointestinal surgeons are usually very familiar with GERD and its treatment.

22. Where can I go for more information about GERD?

If you think you might have GERD - see your doctor who can determine if you have GERD and, if so, can evaluate its severity. Additional information is also available from the following organizations:

The American Gastroenterological Association (AGA)
7910 Woodmont Avenue, 7th Floor
Bethesda, MD 20814
301-654-2055
E-mail the AGA at aga001@aol.com
The American College of Gastroenterology (ACG)
P.O. Box 3099
Alexandria, VA 22302
(703) 820-7400

GERD DEFINED

Gastroesophageal reflux disease (GERD), commonly called chronic heartburn, can significantly impair one's quality of life. Heartburn has nothing to do with the heart; symptoms are caused by stomach acid that backs up (refluxes) into the esophagus, the tube that carries food from the mouth to the stomach. The muscle that separates the stomach and esophagus (called the lower esophageal sphincter, or LES) acts like a one-way valve: it remains closed until swallowing forces it to open and it contracts as soon as the food empties into the stomach. When it does not work properly, stomach acid can reflux into the esophagus and cause the burning sensation of heartburn.

GERD can increase pressure within the abdomen, which may be a factor in the occurrence of hiatal hernias. Approximately 40% of people with GERD also have a hiatal hernia. In most cases, a hiatal, or diaphragmatic, hernia occurs when the lower part of the esophagus and a portion of the stomach slide up through the esophageal hiatus, an opening in the diaphragm through which the esophagus passes before it reaches the stomach. In a small percentage of cases, the junction of the esophagus and stomach remains in place, but a portion of the stomach rolls up and through the esophageal hiatus alongside the esophagus.

A person with GERD and a hiatal hernia generally has more severe reflux and symptoms that are difficult to control with medication and lifestyle changes. When lifestyle changes and/or medication fail to relieve symptoms, a surgical procedure called Nissen fundoplication is used to correct the condition.

Surgical Procedures

Two surgical techniques are employed to perform Nissen fundoplication: open surgery or laparoscopic surgery.

General anesthesia is used to render the patient unconscious. Once the anesthesia has taken effect, the upper abdomen is cleaned with an antiseptic solution to lessen the risk for infection.

In **open surgery**, the surgeon makes a 6- to 10-inch incision in the middle of the abdomen, from just below the ribs to the umbilicus (belly button). If the patient has a hiatal hernia, that is repaired first. The esophageal hiatus is tightened with a couple of stitches to prevent herniation of the fundoplication and then the surgeon performs the procedure.

The upper portion of the stomach (the fundus), which is on the left side of the esophagus, is pulled behind and wrapped around the lower portion of the esophagus and then sutured to the portion of the stomach that has moved into the fundus's original position. This creates a "valve" that acts like the LES to prevent stomach acid from refluxing into the esophagus.

In the **laparoscopic procedure**, the surgeon makes five small incisions in the abdomen. A laparoscope, a miniature telescope attached to a video camera, is inserted through one incision. This allows the surgeon to see the interior of the abdominal cavity. The surgical instruments are inserted through the other incisions. If the patient has a hiatal hernia, that is repaired first. The esophageal hiatus is tightened with a couple of stitches to prevent herniation of the fundoplication and then the surgeon performs the procedure. The fundoplication is performed in the same fashion as in open surgery.

Laparoscopic surgery allows for a faster recovery period, less postoperative pain, a shorter hospital stay, and a much smaller scar.

Whether or not a patient is eligible for laparoscopy depends on several factors and is made on an individual basis. In some circumstances, open surgery is safer.

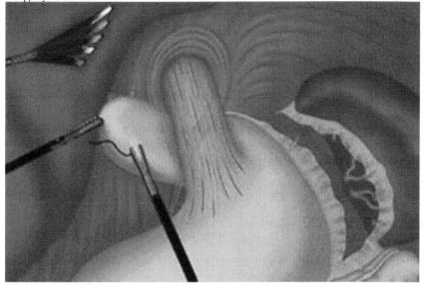

THAT'S NOT THE END OF THE STORY

Just when you probably begun to say to yourself, "So he has a stomach condition", I want to let you know, "that's not the end of story". On 12 March 2003, I was diagnosed as having a Degenerative Disc Disease and a Desiccation of the cervical and lumbar spine multilevel with resulting Parasthesias. To top it all off, I also have was also diagnosed with severe iron deficiency anemia, and a malabsorption syndrome. All of these medical reports came during a two week period. What does that mean to you, the reader in laymen's terms? I'm glad you asked for an explanation.

In order for us to understand what is really taking place in my body, I feel it necessary to give you some definitions to aid in your understanding of the seriousness of the attack of Satan on my body. As a Child of God, it is my belief that God doesn't put illnesses on us, as his children. He will allow them to come upon us although. We'll get back to the subject at hand, but first I want to give you scriptural proof as to what I'm saying.

Let's take a quick look at the second chapter of Job. We have need of picturing ourselves as God saw Job. In the book of Job 2:2-7 it reads:

2 And the Lord said unto Satan, From whence comest thou? And Satan answered the Lord, and said, From going to and fro in the earth, and from walking up and down in it. 3 And the Lord said unto Satan, Hast thou considered my servant Job, that there is none like him in the earth, a perfect and an upright man, one that feareth God, and escheweth evil? And still he holdeth fast his intergrity, although thou movedst me against him, to destroy him without cause. 4 And Satan answered the Lord, and said, Skin for skin, yea, all that a man hath will he give for his life. 5 But put forth thine hand now, and touch his bone and his flesh, and he will curse thee to thy face. 6 And the Lord said unto Satan, Behold, he is in thine hand; but save his life. 7 So went Satan forth from the presence of the Lord, and smote Job with sore boils from the sole of his foot unto his crown.

What God did before Satan, He bragged on Job and his stand. God wanted to know whether or not Satan was convinced, with a shadow of a doubt, that Job was a faithful servant of his. Instead of letting go of his religion, and cursing God, Job held to his faith faster than ever, as that which he has now more than he had need of in ordinary circumstances. Job was the same in adversity, as he was in prosperity. He was far better, and more hearty and lively in blessing God than ever. He took root and held on harder, rather than being shaken by his situation or condition.

God commended Job for his constancy notwithstanding the attacks that were made on him. The Lord continued to brag on Job saying, "Still he holds fast his integrity", as his weapon, and Satan you can't disarm him. Job's belief was more valuable than a chest full of gold and silver in a treasure chest. God spoke of Job with wonder and pleasure because he saw Job triumph in the power of his own grace. The trial of Job was found to his praise and honor.

Even though God said all these things to Satan, that still wasn't convincing enough. He had the nerve to say to God, "Skin for skin, and all that a man has, will he give for his life." For some this may be a truth, because self-love and self-preservation is a very powerful commanding principle in the heart of man. Men love themselves better than their nearest relations, even their children, which are a part of themselves. They will normally do everything to save their own lives. We as people count life as sweet and precious, and while we are in good health and at ease, we can keep trouble from our heart, until trouble comes. We should make a good use of this scriptural proof while God continues to give us our lives, health, and the use of our limbs and senses. We should be the more patient and bear the loss of other comforts in life, as did Job.

Satan had to come to the realization that his hand was too short to truly reach Job the way that he had desired. God did allow him to touch Job, but he wasn't allowed to take his life. We must find ourselves with no less spiritual and mental toughness and stamina that of Job. This is the same strength that I am drawing on, for it was once prophesied to me that I would have the "Spirit of Job". Although Job suffered, he came out victorious. Now let's get back to understanding just what God is allowing me to deal with in my present day life. Again, we'll start off by describing some of my conditions to you, the reader.

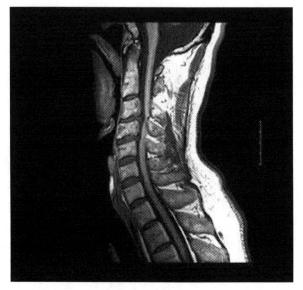

Degenerative Disk Disease

Quick Reference

Reviewed by Dr. Clement J. Cheng

Back pain is one of the most frustrating chronic diseases. Degenerative disk disease is a back disorder that occurs as part of the aging process. It is usually caused by <u>osteoarthritis</u> of the spine, which irritates the vertebrae of the spine with excessive use. When the vertebrae become inflamed due to overuse, they work to heal themselves and leave calcium deposits and bone spurs as side effects. The pain and stiffness that result from this imperfect healing process are known as degenerative disk disease.

Detailed Description

Degenerative disk disease is a general classification including herniated or ruptured disk, prolapsed intervertebral disk, and others.

The disks in the spine are like small sponges that rest between each vertebrae and act as shock absorbers. When <u>arthritis</u> compresses a disk, it tends to bulge out of its alignment; sometimes, it will rupture. When it does, the rupture will usually occur posteriorly. The displaced disk segment may then press on the spinal nerve as it emerges from the spinal cord, or on the cord itself.

A ruptured disk often results in a pinched nerve because of the pressure it puts on nerve tissue. The symptoms that result from a pinched nerve vary according to the location and severity of the injury: a jerking knee, a weak fist, or a numb foot can all be signs of a pinched nerve, and thus, degenerative disk disease.

Diagnosis can be made with simple <u>X-rays</u>. However, if nerve damage is a concern, the doctor may perform an <u>MRI</u> to assess the extent of the damage. Another test to detect a ruptured disk in the lower back is the straight-leg-raise test. The doctor lifts the patient's heel with his or her leg passively extended. This stretches the sciatic nerve, which is located at the back of the hip and goes down the back of the leg. If it elicits pain, the patient probably may have a ruptured disk.

Treatment

Back pain has no easy cure. Some patients usually only treat the symptoms of back pain with heat, rest, and aspirin. Pain relief is essential, because pain causes muscle spasms, which cause more pain, etc. Exercise should be the centerpiece of managing degenerative disk disease. Surgery is used as a last resort.

Next we'll take a brief look at the symptoms typical of degenerative arthritis which involves pain and stiffness when resting, which are reduced in intensity upon becoming physically active. This physical activity must be performed in moderation because excessive bending and lifting tend to exacerbate the symptoms, as does cold, damp weather. When there is referred pain it tends to indicate the presence of nerve root pain and may include muscle spasm and paresthesias with chest and abdominal pain which may simulate visceral disease. The entire spine may be flattened and stiff with limited motion, especially in the lumbar region, where forward bending may be performed primarily by hip motion. Radiographic findings present with loss of articular cartilage from the facets posteriorly and fibrocartilage from the disc anteriorly with secondary bony hypertrophy of the articular cortex.

Maintenance of muscle power, within physiological limits, appears to be the key to retarding degeneration of the spine. A conservative therapeutic regimen in degenerative arthritis includes relief of pain, increased mobility of the spine, with strengthening of the paraspinal musculature. Bed rest includes the use of a firm mattress and may be improved by placing a board between the mattress and box springs to reduce the lumbar lordosis and relieve tension on the articular ligaments. Moist heat may be applied as hot infrared packs, either hydrocollator packs or silicone gel packs, for 15 to 20 minutes, b.i.d., or p.r.n. for pain and/or local spasm. Erythema ab igne must be avoided and the patient must not be allowed to place the heat source under the weight of the body part to avoid capillary compression. Interferential current therapy may be used to reduce pain level and to enhance interstitial fluid transfer serving as a form of massage. Recommended parameters include a 120 Hz beat frequency, with a low grade surging effect if desired, for about 15 to 20 minutes per application, b.i.d., or p.r.n. for pain and/or reduction of edema. Discontinue IFC if the patient finds it intolerable due to sensitivity. Traction may be applied to the cervical, or lumbar, spine and may be used concomitantly. Cervical traction should be applied at an angle of 20 to 30 degrees anterior to the angle of pull in order to enhance IVF patency. Traction may be applied p.r.n. to assist with pain and to enhance mobility. Therapeutic exercise is advisable as soon as acute pain has been controlled, to begin strengthening paraspinal muscles. These exercises must be initiated on a gradual basis beginning with passive effort and gradually building to active exercise without approaching fatigue.

Treatment of spinal degenerative arthritis is ameliorative, rather than curative.

SEVERE IRON DEFICIENCY
IRON DEFICIENCY
Magnitude of the problem

Iron deficiency is a leading cause of anemia, affecting over one-half billion people world wide. Blood loss nearly invariably is the culprit producing iron deficiency in adults. The high demand for iron created by neonatal and adolescent growth spurts occasionally produces iron deficiency in children. Nonetheless, blood loss is the most frequent cause of iron deficiency in this group as well. Body iron stores for women normally vary between one and two grams while men average three to four grams. The liver is the site of most storage iron. Depletion of iron stores precedes impaired production of iron-containing proteins, the most prominent of which is hemoglobin. The two key stages of iron deficiency, are (1) depletion of iron stores without anemia, and (2) depletion of iron stores with anemia. Iron replacement therapy cannot be comfortably undertaken until the cause of the iron deficit is ascertained.

Some disorders disrupt the integrity of the enteric mucosa, thereby hampering iron absorption. Inflammatory bowel disease, particularly Crohn's disease, can injures extensive segments of the small intestine, occasionally extenting to the jejunum and even the duodenum. Invasion of the submucosa by inflammatory cells and disruption of the tissue architecture of the intestine impair iron absorption and uptake of dietary nutrients (Beeken, 1973). Occult gastrointestinal bleeding exacerbates the problem of iron balance. The result is iron deficiency anemia complicated by the anemia of chronic inflammation. Also, Crohn's disease frequently involves the terminal ileum, producing concurrent cobalamin deficiency.

Sprue, both of the tropical and non-tropical variety (celiac disease), can also interfere with iron absorption. Degeneration of the intestinal lining cells along with chronic inflammation causes profound malabsorption. The anemia due to chronic inflammation and iron deficiency often is complicated further by nutritional deficiency. Celiac disease frequently improves dramatically with a gluten-free diet. Some patients with deranged iron absorption lack gross or even histologic changes in the structure of the bowel mucosa. The disease can be mild to the point that it produces few or no symptoms (Corazza et al., 1995). A gluten-free diet improves bowel function in many such patients, with secondary correction of the anemia.

And if those afflictions weren't enough, I've been diagnosed with a rare disease which affects only 4 people in every 10 million persons. This syndrome is known as Zollinger - Ellison syndrome. Here's some medical information to help you to be further educated.

ZOLLINGER-ELLISON SYNDROME; GASTRINOMA

Definition

Zollinger-Ellison syndrome is caused by gastrin-secreting **tumors** of the pancreas that causes severe ulceration (areas of irritation) of the upper gastrointestinal tract (stomach and small bowel).

Causes, incidence, and risk factors

Zollinger-Ellison syndrome is caused by tumors usually found in the head of the pancreas and the upper small bowel. These tumors produce the hormone gastrin and are called gastrinomas. High levels of gastrin cause overproduction of stomach acid.

High acid levels lead to multiple ulcers in the stomach and small bowel. Patients with Zollinger-Ellison syndrome may experience abdominal pain and diarrhea. The diagnosis is also suspected in patients without symptoms who have severe ulceration of the stomach and small bowel.

Gastrinomas may occur as single tumors or as multiple, small tumors. About one-half to two-thirds of single gastrinomas are malignant tumors that most commonly spread to the liver and lymph nodes near the pancreas and small bowel. Nearly 25% of patients with gastrinomas have multiple tumors as part of a condition called multiple endocrine neoplasia type I (MEN I). MEN I patients have tumors in their pituitary gland and parathyroid glands in addition to tumors of the pancreas.

Symptoms

- pain
- vomiting blood (occasional)
- diarrhea

Signs and tests

- The gastrin level is increased.
- A secretin stimulation test is positive.
- A calcium infusion test is positive.
- An abdominal CT scan shows a tumor (or tumors) in the pancreas or early small bowel.
- An octreotide scan shows a tumor in the pancreas or early small bowel.

Treatment

A class of acid-suppressing medications called proton pump inhibitors (for example, omeprazole, lansoprazole) is now first line treatment of Zollinger-Ellison syndrome. These drugs reduce acid production by the stomach dramatically and promote healing of ulcers in the stomach and small bowel. They also provide relief of abdominal pain and diarrhea. Another class of acid-suppressing medications called H-2 blockers may also be used (for example, cimetidine, ranitidine). The H-2 blockers are less potent than proton pump inhibitors.

Surgical removal of a single gastrinoma may be attempted if there is no evidence that it has spread to other organs (such as lymph nodes or the liver). Surgery on the stomach (gastrectomy) to control acid production is rarely necessary today.

Expectations (prognosis)

Early diagnosis and surgical resection is associated with a cure rate of only 20% to 25%.However, gastrinomas are slow growing, and patients may live for many years after the tumor is discovered. Acid-suppressing medications are very effective at controlling the symptoms of acid overproduction.

Complications

- spread of the tumor to other organs (most often liver and lymph nodes)
- failure to locate the tumor during surgery

Calling your health care provider

Call your health care provider if severe, persistent abdominal pain occurs, especially if it occurs with diarrhea.

Chapter Eleven

The Power Of Prayer And Fasting

Here's a story told in scripture, St Matthew 17:14-21, which demonstrates the importance of prayer and fasting. These scriptures will help set the pace for the rest of the chapter. These scriptures refer to the healing of the Demonaic Son.

14 And when they were come to the multitude, there came to him a certain man, kneeling down to him, and saying, 15 Lord, have mercy on my son: for he is lunatick, and sore vexed: for ofttimes he falleth into the fire, and oft into the water. 16 And I brought him to thy disciples, and they could not cure him. 17 Then answered and said, O faithless and perverse generation, how long shall I be with you? How long shall I suffer you? Bring him hither to me. 18 And Jesus rebuked the devil; and he departed out of him: and the child was cured from that very hour. 19 Then came the disciples to Jesus apart, and said, why could not we cast him out? 20 And Jesus said unto them, Because of your unbelief: for verily I say unto you, If ye have faith as a grain of mustard seed, ye shall say unto this mountain, Remove hence to yonder place; and it shall remove; and nothing shall be impossible unto you. 21 Howbeit this kind goeth not out but by prayer and fasting.

These scriptures allowed us to see how important it was for the disciples that walked with Christ to have a measure of faith for themselves, to go along with prayer and fasting, in order to be able to perform the task that was before them. As humans we must realize that we have human weaknesses which are manifested within us that limits what we are or aren't able to do outside of God. We are beings dependent upon God.

Sometimes when we bring our concerns before the Lord through prayer, he may impress a passage of Scripture on your mind. You may not know where to find the scripture, but you may try to find it using a concordance or bible reference dictionary of some sort. A person of God, prayer is interactive when you are in relationship with God. Some people feel they can't concentrate when they a re praying because their minds begin to be filled with Scripture. This is God speaking to you. His Word is living and active. If you are always looking for God to answer your prayer, allow him to speak in any way he chooses. The greatest proof of God's greatest miracles can be found in the Bible. I'm not just speaking concerning the miracles, but I want you to look at the timing of the miraculous events also.

I found that in order for me to get the desired results from God, that I am looking for, I needed to be obedient to his Word. If you expect God to answer your prayers, then you need to take a look at your life and see if it is in agreement with God, as he has shown it to you. After all God has revealed to you through his Word, through your circumstances, and through your relationship wit him, the bottom line to success is always obedience. St John 14:15 tell us, "If ye love me, keep my commandments". Jesus said we are to obey, not wrestle, fight or argue with his Word. Ask yourself, "Am I arguing or fussing with myself or with God about any part of my relationship? Is there anything that is prohibiting you from just obeying? If you find yourself having to fight every time God reveals his Will to you, you might want to do a self examination, and not just for communion's sake.

If you find yourself asking God to prove himself in more than one way or the other, then maybe you don't understand the true meaning of having a personal relationship. I found it helpful when my wife hints that she wants something special, I make my way out to get it for her. That is the same type of relationship God wants us to have with him.

Do we realize what happens when we obey God? When we obey in the least little bit, it sets God in motion on our behalf. He comes alongside us and opens up to our families, our churches, and us.
Let's see what the scriptures say concerning the weaknesses of man, and human weaknesses, which render us needing God in our homes.

Psalm 127:1
Except the Lord build the house, they labour in vain that build it: except the Lord keep the city, the watchman waketh but in vain.
Jeremiah 10:23
O Lord, I know that the way of man is not in himself: it is not in man that walketh to direct his steps.
John 3:27
John answered and said, A man can receive nothing, except it be giving him from heaven.
John 15:5
I am the vine, ye are the branches. He that abideth in me, and I in him, the same bringeth forth much fruit: for without me ye can do nothing.
II Corithians 3:5
Not that we are sufficient of ourselves to think any thing as of ourselves; but our sufficiency is of God;

When we as the Children of God, come to the realization that our total existence is because of God, for God, then and only then will we be able to walk according to his will. I had to understand that it couldn't be done my way. I got tired of hitting my head against a wall or glass that I couldn't see. God allowed me to do things my way until I came to the understanding that it wasn't working. He created us as freethinking individuals, with the ability to make whatever choices in life that we think we are big enough to make. Let's just hope that your choice will be to serve God.

When do we most often call on God? You're right in the time of helplessness. Imagine this that you make a new friend and you can't wait to get to know this person. There is one problem; however, you never speak to them. Whenever you meet, neither of you speak to one another, you just sit quietly from across the room and stare at each other. How long could you go on like this? You will never become friends except you form a meaningful interaction between one another. In other words, you must communicate with one another.

The same is true in developing your relationship with God after you have accepted His Son, Jesus Christ, as your Savior. If you don't ever talk to Him and listen to what He is saying to you, you will miss out on the joy of having a close fellowship and learning more about His character and His love. When you do talk to Him and open your heart to His response, you discover direction and fulfillment that transcends the limits of the human relationship.

Although I have known that prayer was a two-way form of communication, maybe you haven't. In you childhood, prayer may have been a process of reciting words that were told to you. Prayer may have just been a bedtime event for some, which had very little personal meaning. Now that you are an adult you find that there is a significant reason for prayer. Prayer seemed to be something the pastor did on Sunday morning, not an activity designed for you, the individual.

Maybe you don't understand the purpose of prayer, and you have enjoyed it as part of your walk with the Lord for a while. But there are times when prayer is not the dynamic part of your life that you know it can be. Perhaps you did not receive the answer you wanted, or you are not sure if you got an answer at all. You are not confident that you know how to pray, or how to know what God is saying to you in return.

You're not alone, and it's never to late to begin. Don't let anyone tell you that prayer is only for those who have had a relationship with God for a long time. Prayer is for you right where you are today.

Earlier we spoke about helpless moments, so let's take a quick look at some physical and spiritual moments when God was needed. You just might find yourself in one of these situations. These scriptures should allow you to know that prayer works, and it will let you know why you should pray.

Luke 13:11

And, behold, there was a woman which had a spirit of infirmity eighteen years, and was bowed together, and could in no wise lift up herself.

Having a severe acid reflux as an infirmity for over thirteen years myself, I can relate to this womans condition. At times all I can do is to roll over in a ball and hold my stomach. Even after all the surgeries', I still am having problems with my stomach, so my total dependence is in God for total healing.

St John 5:7

The impotent man answered him, Sir, I have no man, when the water is troubled, to put me into the pool: but, while I am coming, another stepped down before me.

St John 6:44

No man can come to me, except the Father hath sent me draw him: and I will raise him up at the last day.

Acts 3:2

And a certain man lame from his mother's womb was carried, whom they laid daily at the gate of the temple which is called Beautiful, to ask alms of them that entered into the temple;

Romans 5:6

For when we were yet without strength, in due time Christ died for the ungodly.

Romans 7:18

For I know that in me (that is, in my flesh,) dwelleth no good thing: for to will is present with me; but how to perform that which is good I find not.

Because of man's extremity of weakness, God has an opportunity to help us in our everyday lives. So you ask why should you pray? The primary reason is to establish a relationship with God. Prayer is essentially a conversation with God in which you praise Him, thank Him for His blessings, and tell Him what is on your heart and mind. In the process, God speaks to you through His Word, by the Holy Spirit, and others, a pastor or trusted Christian friend.

God commands us to pray. Philippians 4:6-7 says,

6 "Be anxious for nothing, but in everything by prayer and supplication with thanksgiving let your requests be made known to God. 7 And the peace of God, which surpasses all   comprehension, shall guard your hearts and your minds in Christ Jesus."

Prayer is not a burdensome responsibility for the believer; it is a joy and privilege. Each day, you can talk to the God who created everything in existence. He is all-powerful and all knowing. Nothing can remove you from His loving presence, and He wants you to share every aspect of your existence with Him. I have found it to be a wonderful experience praying to God through words or in by the means of tongues.

Prayer gives you the proper understanding of your position as God's child and an awareness of His involvement in your life. When you bring Him your problems, cares, and anxieties, what you are acknowledging is this:

God, I need You. I don't have the answers, but I know You do." This is an expression of total dependence on Him, and it is humbling. But recognizing the Lord's power and sufficiency in all things is key to experiencing His security and abundant provision.

When Should You Pray

Many believers, even when they recognize the importance of praying, feel that they don't pray often enough. They pray when they are in trouble or have a pressing need, but when the pressure slacks off, so does their diligence.

Here's what usually happens, pain or hardship drives us to our knees in a hurry, but somehow in peaceful times the motivation to come before God seems to linger far behind. Apostle Paul discussed this tendency in his letter to the Thessalonians, who were struggling hard against the worldly influences around them.

I Thessalonians 5:16-18
"Rejoice always; pray without ceasing, in everything give thanks; for this is God's will concerning you in Christ Jesus".

What does it mean to pray without ceasing? Does he mean that you must be voicing a prayer out loud or in your head every waking moment? No, of course not, but don't miss what Paul is saying. The point here is priority; time with God in prayer should be number one. It should be the first in your heart and mind. Nothing else comes before spending time with Him.

Jesus made it clear that prayer is the most important part of fellowship with God. When He was on this earth, He spent much time alone talking with the Father (Luke 5:16). The crowds gathered around Him; the disciples needed His attention. Yet even with all the demands of His time and physical energy, He made communing with God His foremost activity. The Lord says in Proverbs 8:17:

16 I love them that love me; and those that seek me early shall find me.

Colossians 4:2-4
2 "Continue in prayer, and watch in the same with thanksgiving; 3 Withal praying also for us that God would open unto us a door of utterance, to speak the mystery of Christ, for which I am also in bonds: 4 That I may make it manifest, as I ought to speak.

God will give you what and when to say at the appointed time, just by seeking Him early and finding Him. One should remain in constant attention and perseverance continually in prayer to the leading of the Lord.

As you go through the day, lift up the needs and problems you encounter. When and if a task goes well then thank God for his help. If you are on your way to a meeting, ask Him to prepare your mind and give you clarity and insight. Share with Him all of your experiences and learn to rely on His guidance. Ephesians 5:19 remind us that we are to go about "speaking to one another in psalms and hymns and spiritual songs, singing and making melody with your heart to the Lord." Prayer is more than just an activity; it is to be a continual mind-set and all-pervasive attitude.

Prayer should be a regular part of your everyday life. Few things in life are more upsetting than knowing how important prayer is and then not doing it. We have all struggled in this area of commitment, but until we join the Lord in heaven, we must continue diligently seeking a process of communication with Him.

So what if you have a different way of praying, you have a least made a commitment to pray. Continue to commit to praying a certain number of minutes everyday to build up your prayer life. Keep a watching eye out for the prayer obstacles; skipping a day or two, or the old phone-ringing trick. You never know what the reason will be for your slipping from day to day when it comes to your spending quality time with the Lord. There are some practical ways to fight the clamor of the day and find consistent victory and joy in prayer. First, you need to seta a specific time to pray, like early in the morning about 5 o'clock a.m. Make an "appointment" with the Lord and even write it down on your schedule for the day. It sounds silly doesn't it, but just think you make appointments with your doctor. Isn't Jesus more important? When prayer is a planned event, you can take the necessary precautions to protect that time.

Be careful not to fall into that clock punching mentality, because then you put prayer in an organized sequence of events, rather than it being a personal intimate time spent with God. Don't allow yourself to feel tat you are making arrangements for a special encounter with God; your anticipation for your special moments will grow over time, more and more.

The next thing to do is to find a location or secret closet. Yes you can pray anywhere and at anytime, but when you have one chosen place, it becomes a personal sanctuary. That place can be a special room or nook or closet or chair in the corner, wherever you are the most free from avoidable distractions.

Next I would write your prayers in a journal or notebook. Put the date at the end of each one; and when God answers, draw a single line through the request so you can still read it. Record the answer date at the end of the line, and as you review the pages, you can rejoice at His provision. You will say, "God loves me. He is interested in me. I am growing in my faith, and He is actively involved in my life." The excitement of this review process is unbeatable.

Keep Your Prayer Specific

When you pray vaguely or indefinite prayers, you show that the request does not mean very much to you. Otherwise, you would take the time to think it through and verbalize the details. Anything less is like gong into a restaurant and ordering "food and drink." You need to state the desires of your heart with exactness so you will know when God has answered and so He receives the glory.

God insists that we ask, not because He needs to know our situation, but because we need the spiritual discipline of asking. Similarly, making our requests specific forces us to take a step forward in faith. The reason many of us retreat into vague generalities when we pray is not because we think too highly of God, but because we think too little. If we pray for something definite and our request is not granted, we fear to lose the little faith we had. So we fall back on the safe route of highly, "spiritual" prayers, the kind that Jesus brushed aside as not true prayer at all, just self-deceptive "talking to ourselves." We also must add another ingredient to prayer and that is fasting.

Prayer and Fasting

This is where the power is at, because fasting puts us in harmony with an all powerful God who demands humility from those who wish to be close to Him. Fasting humbles the flesh. When it is dome for that purpose, it pleases the Spirit of God.

You can go a certain distance in God, and experience many things, without fasting much, but the highest, richest and most powerful blessings always go to those who together with other disciplines, fast much unto God. The most significant Biblical characters, with the possible exception of Abraham, were all men of fasting and prayer (Matthew 4:2). So was the apostle Paul (2 Corinthians 11:27). Moses fasted 80 days. Elijah fasted 40 days as well as did I, closing out one year and starting the next. The early church fasted before starting any major work. The greatest spiritual leaders of the 20th century who are making an impact are all men of fasting of prayer to my knowledge. Anyone who started a significant spiritual movement in Christianity was, to the best of my knowledge Luther, Wesley, Finney, Booth were all men of fasting. In our day, Cho, Bonnke, Osborn, Annacondia are all men of much fasting. If done right, fasting counts a lot with God.

Fasting is not magic; it doesn't it twist the arm of God. God wants to do many amazing things, but He looks for those willing to urgently make the corrections needed to come into line with him. God resists the proud, but gives grace to the humble. Successful fasting is also the fastest way to learn patience. As I journeyed into my 40-day fasting experience in Kuwait, I had to yet work daily and yet maintain my patience and discipline when dealing with others. God allowed me to see things in my self-daily that I didn't particularly like. There were attitudinal changes that needed to be made. I had no other alternative but to change if I wanted to walk obediently in God. It took patience and endurance to fast for more than one day. I endured many test daily as I fasted, but the quicker the test came allowed me to have better opportunities to past them. If I wanted to go far with God I would have to face these test anyway; it might have been much later, and in a more time consuming and difficult manner. We need to "bite the bullet" and embrace the correction God wants to apply our souls.

Fasting gives you God's focus for your life. It is a major key to hearing God's voice (the other is true worship - the two are related). We need focus from God more than anything. The world we live in is working overtime to distract us, to entice us, to win our hearts and minds, our focus, and to determine our vision. Fasting cuts out the world so we can tune into God. If we are obedient to God fasting will make us catalysts for revival and awakening.

The Pain of Fasting

Fasting is not easy. There are degrees of fasting, of course. The pain of fasting is twofold. The physical pain is due to the detoxification of our bodies. All the accumulate poison and garbage starts to come into our blood and we feel dreadful. Fasting on juice can alleviate this. With juice fasting you have some control on the speed of your body's detoxification.

The soulish pain is due to the conflict in the spiritual realm between your flesh and the Spirit of God. This goes behind the natural desire to eat. There is soulish pain because most times our bodies are demanding food 3 times a day and complain that food is needed when it is denied. A little training in fasting soon clears up those problems. You cannot use food as an emotional crutch to give pleasure, drowsiness, satisfaction and escape. Instead you must depend on God for comfort. You very well may be brought face to face with other painful issues in your life, which is the time for you to deal with them. God may reveal the need for you to forgive others, to repent of your wicked ways, to stop running from Him and start trusting Him. There is thus also a spiritual and soulish detoxification, which happens when we fast.

Here's a short testimony that I want to share with you the reader. As I was going through my 40 day fast, God showed me a lot of things about myself that I needed to change. I never had a positive relationship with my father, and I never respected him as my father figure. I had so much hatred or disappointment built up inside of me, because I saw myself having a willingness to be a father, when I myself never had one. There was no way that I could escape my responsibilities as a man, husband or father, yet somehow this man was able to do it. To make matters worst, I had the responsibility of taking care of another man's son. I was unable or unwilling to see what God was trying to show me and understand where he continues to take me in him. When the Word of God tells us that all things work together for our good, it really does. God restored my relationship with my wife, children, father and brother, because I had a willingness to do things God's way. It took my being obedient to God in proceeding on this fast, especially for that length of time, and being deployed oversees while dealing with the medical conditions that I was encountering at that particular time.

There is an absolute possibility that you will be attacked by demonic forces seeking to induce you to give up the fast. Jesus experienced this in the wilderness with Satan (Matthew 4:1-10). Great spiritual victories are won or lost on our willingness to endure spiritual hardship and temptation out of love and faithfulness to the lord. You will experience weakness at times, and we like to feel strong and in control. Fasting teaches us dependence upon God. In sharing this information with you on this subject, please join everyone that believes in fasting and God, and pray for each other that God will strengthen us in our resolve to let Him teach us to wait upon Him with fasting, prayer and the Word.

Chapter Twelve

Waiting After The Wait

Man not that word again, WAIT! How many times in our life have we heard someone say that to us; wait on this, or wait on that? This sounds like a never-ending saga or word that just cringes in our inner being. Isn't there another word in the English vocabulary other than this one? Why would the Lord allow this word to be introduced to us? The words that we like to hear most of all is yes and right now. This word better suits what our flesh desires. When we have to wait it costs us something, ourselves.

Why does this four-letter word cause us so much turmoil? Let's take a quick look at this word, which causes us to be so easily disturbed. The word *wait* is defined as:

1. a. To postpone action or stay I one spot until something anticipated occurs. b. To linger until another catches up. 2. To remain or be in readiness or expectation. 3. To remain temporarily neglected or postponed. 4. To work as a waiter or waitress. Vt., to remain or stay in expectation of.

Look at this definition; all it does is tell us that we can't have what we want right now. This word doesn't even have audacity to tell us why. That's not good enough, we need a reason for why we can't have it, so here it is; cause it's not your season. Yes, I know that's not grammatically correct, but you get the jest of what I am saying. Yes, my friend Maxine too reminded me once, "It's just not your season yet". As a reminder to my spirit man, and a source of torment to my flesh, Ecclesiastes 3:1-8, states:

To every thing there is a season, and a time to every purpose under the heaven: 2 A time to be born, and a time to die; a time to plant, and a time to pluck up that which is planted; 3 A time to kill, and a time to heal; a time to break down, and a time to build up; 4 A time to weep, and a time to laugh; a time to mourn, and a time to dance; 5 A time to cast away stone, and a time to gather stones together; a time to embrace, and a time to refrain from embracing; 6 A time to get, and a time to lose; a time to keep, and a time to cast away; 7 A time to rend, and a time to sew; a time to keep silence, and a time to speak; 8 A time to love, and a time to hate; a time of war, and a time of peace.

So now we should understand the reasoning behind our having to **WAIT!** It seems to serve it's designed purpose. There is a preparation period needed for us to get everything that is required to complete the specific task, which will be given unto us by God. In the book of Roman 8:25, we are instructed and encouraged as to why we should wait:

25 But if we *hope* for that we see not, then do we *with patience* wait for it.

God hasn't left us without an answer to the question that may have entered our minds. So, be strong in the Lord and in the power of His might, as you with patience. The preceding verse tells us that when we see that which we are looking for, then we are not hoping for it, or why would we hope for it? It is there and it can be touched, so there would no need of waiting. There is an old cliché that says, "Anything worth having is worth waiting for". I know, you never heard that one.

Maybe just like you, I'm waiting for a lot of things. I'm waiting for my change to come spiritually (ministry wise), financially and militarily.

It seems so very hard, especially when you have been going through for as long as I have, but I have to remember to trust the Lord, and wait patiently on Him. During the waiting process it is possible to get three answers from God; yes, no or not now. In Philippians 4:11 Paul states:

11 Not that I speak in respect of want: for I have learned, in whatsoever state that I am, therewith be content.

Paul's contentment allowed him to have the victory over anxiety. For the Word of God tells us not to be anxious for anything. Think about this, when your anxious, you are uneasy in your mind. You must be earnestly wishing for something. Your uneasiness can lead to your becoming awkward and embarrassed. It also causes you to be disturbed by pain or worry. Your mind becomes restless, and you will likely be lacking in stability and certainty. Do you really want to be in this state described here? I know I wouldn't, now that I see what I would be doing to myself.

One of the things that makes one anxious, is knowing what the Lord has shown you that He has for you to do, and you don't know how your going to get there. The Word of God encourages us with at least two scriptures, Philippians 4:6-7:

6 Be careful for nothing; but in every thing by prayer and supplication with thanksgiving let your requests be made known unto God. 7 And the peace of God, which passeth all understanding, shall keep your hearts and minds through Christ Jesus.

Here's a remedy for our unrest. We must not only keep up scheduled times for prayer, but we must pray when emergencies arise. The phrase, " In every thing by prayer", let's us know that when anything burdens our spirits, we must ease our minds by prayer. When our situations are perplexed or distressed, we must seek direction and support from God. We must join thanksgiving with our prayers and supplications. We must not only seek supplies of good, but we must own receipts of mercy. Prayer is a source of offering up our desires to God, or making them known to him. Letting your requests be made known to God is a crucial step also. It is not that God needs to be told about either your wants or desires, He already knows them better than we can tell Him. This process allows Him to know them better from us, and it gives us an opportunity to show our regards and concern. It also expresses our value of the mercy and sense of our dependence on him. The effect of this will be the peace of God keeping our heart.

The peace of God is the comfortable sense of our reconciliation to God and interest in his favor, and the hope of the heavenly blessedness, and enjoyment of God. The phrase," which passeth all understanding", is a greater good than can be sufficiently valued or duly expressed.

One of the problems that I saw within myself was the need to always be achieving. I could never find self-satisfaction in anything that I was doing. It seemed as though my military career had taken a turn for the worst. I have been a Staff Sergeant in the United States military for 6 years, and I didn't understand. I had become so unease and depressed about my lack of progression, that I had forgotten all the things that were really important, God and my family. It was important for me to achieve goals that I had set for myself immediately, or I felt that I was a failure. I didn't have the desire to wait on the Lord. I would become easily depressed and doubtful. My goal was being promoted within the first two years after being promoted to Staff Sergeant.

The irony of it all is that I found out, I believe, the reason why I hadn't gotten promoted to Sergeant First Class. I heard myself speaking to another soldier that if and when I got promoted, no would be able to do anything to me. The Spirit of God quickly let me know that was the reason why I hadn't gotten promoted. It all came down to my attitude. Through it all, I had to learn not only how to wait on the Lord, but I had to have the correct attitude while waiting. I also had to be of good courage, and know that I shouldn't be weary in well doing, for I would reap if I fainted not. So now I know that whatever I do in word or in deed, I need to do it as unto the Lord.

Although I had been shown a vision of what was to come at the age of 13 to 16, I had to do the inevitable, so I thought, I had to wait. Habakkuk 2:1-4 has encouraged me by letting me know that I should wait.

1 I will stand upon my watch, and set me upon the tower, and will watch to see what he will say unto me, and what I shall answer when I am reproved. 2 And the Lord answered me, and said, Write the vision, and make it plain upon tables, that he may run that readeth it. 3 For the vision is yet for an appointed time, but at the end it shall speak, and not lie: though it tarry, wait for it; because it will surely come, it will not tarry. 4. Behold, his soul which is lifted up is not upright in him; but the just shall live by his faith.

This should encourage any man, woman, boy or girl to trust in the Lord, despite what you see. Know that it is not by your power, or by your might, but it is by God's Spirit says the Lord. This very thing happened to me while I pulling Division EOC duty while stationed in Fort Stewart, Ga. On 15 May 2002, the Lord spoke to me and told me to sit down and draw my vision on paper. About a month or so later I showed the drawing to my pastor, and he said, "Jones, this is doable". In August of the same year, I spoke to Reverend Williams, one of the leaders of the jail ministry, the drawing and he got so excited. He said that he and another sister were given a vision along this line. It was nine months later, and we have begun to make all of our visions a reality. Here's an important key although, we are first following the vision of the leader appointed over us, our pastor. Don't get discouraged; in following the vision of the Shepard, the sheep get fed their visions share also.

Here's a short testimony, which will demonstrate why it is important to wait on the Lord. I went to a business meeting, and while in this particular meeting, someone mentioned the possibility of employing a certain group of people. Now the people in this meeting had no idea that I wanted to employ this type of persons, but God knows exactly what we need. God knew that these personnel would be in need of employment, so He's supplying there need as well as fulfilling the vision. When God gives you a vision and a mission, He will supply the means to complete the task. The whole point to this testimony, is when we wait on God, your season will come, if you faint not.

Has my season finally come? I received a phone call from a fellow minister from the church. He has been given the task of running the jail ministry for our church, but he is currently occupied with some other things in his life. He called me tonight to let me know that he was going to talk with the pastor concerning him allowing me to run this particular ministry. The question that keeps popping up in my mind is, why didn't the pastor ask me to run the ministry when he knew this was an area in which I believe I am called to work in? I had spoken to him concerning the vision that I had which pertained to this type of ministry, yet he chose someone else. I had to remind myself that it is not about me anyway, it is about God's business, and He alone should get the glory. I am just thankful that I was considered as person to operate in this area of ministry. We haven't yet spoken with the pastor; this is to take place this Friday.

Friday has come and gone, but no meeting has taken place concerning what is to come with the jail ministry. I have although, begun to travel with the brethren to the youth detention center. I see the young boys being held in this place, and it troubles my spirit that the majority of the youth are African American males. I hate to see any of the youth incarcerated. What this means is that we have not meet the need of these youth. We the community or village of people are also responsible for the upbringing of the youth in our perspective neighborhoods.

A 92-year-old young man, as Pastor Jackson called him, shared a word of God with us, coming from St John 5:1-12. This story will teach us a few of life's lesson. One story that is pertinent to this chapter is the length of waiting period, after the wait. This chapter tells us of a man who had a certain infirmity thirty-eight years, but he never could make it to the pool known as, "Bethesda. This pool had five porches, and was stirred or troubled by an angel. The significance of the pool was that whoever stepped in the water first after the troubling of the water, was made whole of whatsoever disease he had. Let's read what the scriptures had to say, starting at verse six:

6 When Jesus saw him lie, and knew that he had been now a long time in that case, he saith unto him, Will thou be made whole? 7 The impotent man answered him, Sir, I have no man, when the water is troubled, to put me into the pool: but while I am coming, another steppeth down before me. 8 Jesus saith unto him, Rise, take up thy bed and walk. 9 And immediately the man was made whole, and took up his bed, and walked: and on the same day was

the Sabbath. 10 The Jews therefore said unto him that was cure, It is the Sabbath day: it is not lawful for thee to carry thy bed. 11 He answered them, He that made me whole, the same said unto me, Take up thy bed, and walk. 12 Then asked they him, What man is that which said unto thee, Take up thy bed, and walk?

In this grouping of scripture, the first thing we see is that the man with the infirmity had been in this condition for a long time. He had been waiting for his change to come, but he couldn't get to the true source of help. This should be a source of encouragement for all of us. When Christ came up to Jerusalem he visited not the palaces, but the hospitals, which demonstrated one instance of his humility, and condescension, and tender compassion towards others. This was an indication of his great design in coming into the world, which was to seek and save the sick and wounded.

Although there was a great multitude of poor cripples here at Bethesda, Christ fastened his eyes upon this one, and singled him out from the rest. Was it because he was the oldest person in the house, or the one who was in the worst shape? Only Jesus himself knows why he chose this particular man. Jesus delights to help the helpless, and hath mercy on whom he will have mercy. One thing is certain; Jesus considered how long the man had lain in this condition. Those who have been long in affliction may comfort them with this, that God keeps account of how long we have been in suffering.

Just as the man was asked the question, Wilt thou be made whole, God says the same thing to us. It may seem to be a strange question to ask ourselves, especially if we, like the man, have been ill so long. These illnesses can be of spiritual or natural natures. The key is for us not to be satisfied in the unwanted state that we may find ourselves in. The man said when he was coming to the pool; another person stepped in before him. We too may have felt in times past, felt despaired and disappointed, and then Jesus will step in and give us relief. He delights to help in desperate cases.

We are learning how to be thankful for the least bit of kindness. We are also being taught how to be patient under the greatest contempt's. We may let our resentments be ever so just, but our expressions should ever be so calm. It probably seemed to the man that he was waiting in vain, yet still he continued lying by the pool-side, hoping some time or the other, help would come.

While we find ourselves in verse eight of this chapter, we observe Christ not biding the man to rise and go into the waters, but rise and walk. He had tapped into the right source of help after, "waiting after the wait". Christ did that for us, which the law could not do, and set that aside. A point that needs to be made is, first it is a perfect cure and miraculous. The man did not recover strength by degrees, but from the extremity of weakness and impotency he suddenly stepped into the highest degree of bodily strength. Secondly, after Christ had cured him, he had to proclaim the cure. He went a step further by proclaiming it to the public. When we have wanted a long time for our change to come, we should be happy to tell someone about it.

Just as it was for the man, it will be a joyful surprise to us that are spiritually crippled, to find ourselves all of a sudden so strong and able to help ourselves. Nothing is to hard for Christ to do. We to, like the man, have to obey the power of Christ's word commanding us to rise up from our situations, and then walk with him.

The man, after being questioned by the Jews, justified his working on the Sabbath, by saying, " He that made me whole, the same said unto me, Take up they bed, and walk". He told them that he did not do it in contempt of the law and the Sabbath, but in obedience to the one who, by making him whole, had given him undeniable proof that he is greater than either of them or the law. He believed that a person who could work such a miracle as make him whole, no doubt might have given him such a command as to carry his bed. He that could overrule the powers of nature, no doubt might overrule a positive law, especially in an instance not of the essence of the law. When we find ourselves having to choose between obeying God and man, always choose to obey God. Don't fear those that can only destroy your body, for God can destroy both your body and your soul.

The conclusion to the whole matter is this, no matter how long you have waited after the wait, trusts God. You may not know how long of a wait you're going have, just know that God is in control of your life. Many people don't know Christ as their Lord and Savior, but he has worked a lot of issues out for them. The man didn't even know who did the healing, but he recognized the power and authority that Christ possessed. Trust in the Lord, and lean not to your own understanding.

Chapter Thirteen

My Husband And I

Well, well, well, I guess it's my turn to tell you about this man. There is so much to say, but in so little space to write it in. It hasn't been easy, but with God in his life it so much better. God truly makes a difference when it comes to the "Making of A Man". I have seen both the bad and the good in this man, but I know this very thing, he is a true Man of God. My husband loves the Lord with all his heart, soul and his mind. He endeavors to do God's will both here and abroad. He is a man that prays, fasts and seeks after God's heart. He has and is yet being tested by the fire, but he is determined to hear the Word of the Lord say,

"Well done, thou good and faithful servant: thou hast been faithful over a few things, I will make thee ruler over many things: enter thou into the joy of they Lord."

All the things that we have gone through to get to the point have been worth the pain. Don't get me wrong; I didn't enjoy suffering through the heartaches and disappointments, but after seeing what God has done in his life, I thank God for God.

Now I can share with you how God got us to this place and time. I met my born-again, handsome, wonderful, and darling husband some eight plus years ago in Harker Heights, Texas. I was attending a revival at our church in September of 1994, being run by Bishop Arthur

Ladell Thomas, our pastor and jurisdictional bishop. It was a Sunday night, and in comes walking this fine brother; to me of course. He immediately got my attention, although he didn't know it at the time. Before I get to the rest of the story, I want to let you know that there is an ironic twist to this story. It had been prophesied to me, a week prior that I would be marrying a preacher. Now I know that things don't just happen in our lives. God has already preordained what he has for us in our lives. It is up to us to get to that point through the following of His divine plan. Moving on with the story, in comes walking this brother and "pow", I was knocked off my feet.

I didn't get to speak to him on his first night of the revival, but he came back on the next night. I knew I had to move quickly so I wrote my name on a piece of paper, as to get his attention; and I did. Here's twist number one, my son got to the paper before he had a chance to get it. I didn't give up though, for I knew I had to meet this guy personally. I was afforded another opportunity later. We were going to have a single's meeting and he and another preacher were going to be sharing their experiences pertaining to marriage, but I had other ideas. I want to you first to understand that I am in no way condoning or glorifying sin, that's just the state that I was in. I came to church intentionally, with this African pride dress on that fit every curb I had perfectly. It worked like a charm, because I got his attention so well that he ran out of the church. He had to go and tell God that he didn't come all the way to Texas for this, meaning to fall into sin. Later on he told me how fine and beautiful looking I appeared in my dress. He had to repent for his sin, because I was so fine to him. He wanted me as much as I wanted him. Love didn't have anything to do with it. Again, I am not advocating sin, I'm just telling the story, because we know that the Word of the Lord tells us, "For the wages of sin is death, but the gift of God is eternal life.

As you probably figured out by now, we exchanged personal information and eventually went out to lunch together. It now came for the time for him to leave the reception station, a place where all incoming soldiers live momentarily, before reporting to their new units. When he got to his new battalion, 1/67 Armored Battalion, they didn't have barracks space for him to occupy. Neither did they want him to go and get a room off post, so after he was asked did he have a place he could stay for the weekend, I volunteered my services. I told him he could stay at my place for the weekend; and he did. I took him to my place for the weekend and the next thing you know, we were married within ten days after meeting each other.

I know the bible says in Proverbs 18:22, "Whoso findeth a wife findeth a good thing, and obtaineth favour of the Lord", but that was quick, don't you think. It happened so fast that I don't think we realized what really happened. Then the test of marriage begun, he had his old baggage and so did I. We hadn't really resolved many of our old issues, before we had a chance to begin dealing with our new ones. I had to deal with his old affairs and new ones. It was heart breaking and disappointing. When I saw him as a preacher, I had a totally different perspective of what or who I thought he was to be. I forgot that he was human. He was and is just a man striving to live right, just like I am attempting to do. One lesson that I learned is that you can't put to high an expectation on anyone that you yourself know that they won't be able to reach.

On the day of our marriage we got hit by a van, while attempting to leave Walmart's shopping center, which by the way is still our favorite place to shop. Murphy's Law didn't stop there, as life often does, my husband had to go to the NTC (National Training Center), in California after only being married to me for less than a month. I then came down on orders for Korea. I had to report to Korea by January of 1995. Now picture this scenario, a new couple with a child, and a man who is a now a stepfather and a wife on her way to Korea. What does that spell? It spelled trouble. I had to leave my son with a man that I didn't really know, and what was worst, one that my son didn't know either. There was nothing that I could do but leave them both to each other. Of course, you probably figured it out; it didn't work out well at all.

Without getting into every detail of my life, I want to tell you that I went through the hurts and pains of his being unfaithful to me. Although I never caught him, he was foolish enough to tell me about it. He learned his lesson. He learned that God intended for him to be the husband of one wife. He was and is the head of our family. He is the priest and provider of our home. We have relinquished our control of this marriage and given it over to God, and He has given it back to us renewed and in tact. That is what God will do when you only trust in Him as your Lord and Savior.

Hold on the story is not over. There are some lessons to be learned here in this chapter as well as throughout this book. One key element is that there is a difference between forgiveness and reconciliation. We must define these two words in order for you, the reader, to see what God is showing in my husband's book.

Forgiveness - is the releasing of a person's debt. Most New Testament occurrences are translations from the Greek word "aphamey" which means to cut off, let loose, pardon. Forgiveness is in the power of the wounded regardless of the attitude, behavior, or wishes of the wounder or debtor. Forgiveness releases the wounded to move on with their lives.

Reconciliation - is not in the power of the wounded. Reconciliation I requires genuine remorse, repentance, and heart change from the life of the offender/debtor. Until this posture is taken by the wounder, the wounded cannot administer reconciliation. These two concepts are often mistakenly interchanged. People can genuinely forgive an act against them and never have a relationship with the offender.

This is not the case with my husband and me. God has allowed our marriage to become better than before. I'm not saying our marriage is without trials and tribulations, but we have learned to trust and seek God. Most importantly, God has allowed us to see one another, and not just our own selfish desires.

If you can remember this, God has given man certain responsibilities, certain things to do and not to do. Every man has failed at some point to do what he should or shouldn't have done. Sin is universal. Everyone fails in his duty at some point to some degree. Everyone needs to pray "forgive us our debts, as we forgive our debtors."

The last thing that I want to leave with you is found in two forms of thoughts in these few scriptures (1 John 1:9, Isaiah 55:7, Jeremiah 33:8) and (Mark 11:25, Luke 17:4, Ephesian 4;32, and Colossian 3:13) for it will save not only your marriage but your soul from a burning Hell.

Thought 1.   "Forgive us our debts, as we forgive our debtors" is the fourth request to be prayed. The believer should pray "after this manner."

1) "Father, forgive me-have mercy upon me, the sinner, the nothing. O'God , You are all, and please have mercy.

2) "Father, forgive others of all their sins. I hold nothing within. O'God, if there is anything within my heart against anyone, help me to forgive.

Thought 2. In seeking forgiveness we have a duty to God and to man.

1) Our duty to God is to ask forgiveness when we fail to do His will.

"If we confess our sins, he is faithful and just to forgive us our sins, and to cleanse us from all unrighteousness" (1 John 1:9)

"Let the wicked forsake his way, and the unrighteous man his thoughts: and let him return unto the Lord, and he will have mercy upon him; and to our God, for he will abundantly pardon" (Isaiah 55:7).

"And I will cleanse them from all their iniquity, whereby they have sinned against me; and I will pardon all their iniquities, whereby they have sinned, and whereby they have transgressed against me" (Jeremiah 33:8).

2) Our duty to man is to forgive his sins against us.

"And when ye stand praying, forgive, if ye have ought against any: that your Father also which is in heaven may forgive you your trespasses" (Mark 11:25).

"And if he trespass against thee seven times in a day, and seven times in a day turn again to thee, saying, I repent; thou shalt for give him" (Luke 17:4).

"And be ye kind one to another, tenderhearted, forgiving one another, even as God for Christ's sake hath for given you" (Ephesians 4:32).

"Forbearing one another, and forgiving one another, if any man have a quarrel against any: even as Christ forgave you. So also do ye" (Colossians 3:13).

If we wish to be forgiven ourselves, both duties have to be performed. We must forgive those who sin against us (Matthew 6:12), and we must ask forgiveness for our sins (1 John 1:9). This was the key element that my husband and I learned in life, as we sought after God. These elements allowed my husband to be the Man of God that God has intended for him to be. This is how this book, "The Making of A Man" came to be a reality.

Responsible

You need to be more responsible
They all proclaimed
But far from me, responsibility remained

But how do I get there
I just couldn't see
Why responsibility has remained so far from me

You need to be more responsible
I was often told
You're a grown man
You're forty something years old

This thing called responsibility
Is really important too, I see
It's not only needful for you, but also for me

The message was made very clear
It went to my mind and my heart
I asked the Lord to make me more responsible
And give me a brand new start

Michael L. Jones Sr. – author 09/24/07

Chapter Fourteen

Getting My House In Order

The most important element needed in "getting my house in order" was for me to be become more responsible. I found that what I lacked most, in my being made into a man and my bearing my cross was my being more responsible. The poem entitled "Responsible" spoke the sentiments of this subject as it pertains to the final stages of my being complete as a "Totally responsible man of God".

This concept was not foreign to me, but knowing how to get there was. I couldn't see the importance of it for the most part of my life. It took my going through the last stages of my life to understand how my lack of responsibility had totally affected my life. I had been irresponsible, first to God, my ex-wife and all my children. I had been irresponsible in my finances also which led to my having credit problems. But the good thing about it all, is knowing that it didn't have to remain that way.

What I found most puzzling was how to know what is really expected of me as a man, by God, as it pertained to getting my house in order. What was equally important was that I didn't have to try and measure myself up against another man. What really mattered was whether I lived up to the expectations of God. What I needed to demonstrate in my life was ability to demonstrate **masculine distinction, servant leadership, and spiritual equality which show a sign of strength in character**.

Oftentimes I felt confused because of all the pain that was associated with being "a man" and the expectations of being responsible along with it. Somewhere in my mind I felt that the one's that were responsible for my well being weren't. But what I found out was that it is critical for a man to know what to expect of himself, as well as how to deal with the unrealistic and conflicting expectations of others.

In order for me to be made into a "responsible man" I had to truly understand where God fell into all of this. What was and is His expectation of me as a responsible man? I was blessed to find out that the Bible had all the answers for questions and people who were and are confused like myself. The Bible provides high standards, but reasonable expectations. It also provides help and wisdom from God, who offers His presence and encourages both men and women to learn from Him. We are able to draw on His strength and we can also seek out His guidance.

ROLE CONTRADICTION

I spoke of three areas above, masculine distinction, servant leadership and spiritual equality; all which show a sign of strength in character. To some men, servant leadership sounds as crazy as drinking warm water on a hot day. How can you be a servant and a leader at the same time? Leadership doesn't always mean to be in control. Neither does your being a servant mean that you are subservient in nature. The Bible's definition of leadership is for a man to be responsible, compassionate, understanding, accountable, competent, respectable, authoritative, pioneering, exemplary, and God-fearing.

As a man and a leader, I learned that I didn't have to make all the decisions in a relationship. Nor did it mean that I had to be the "boss" in my marriage, at church or in society at large. All I needed to do was to take the initiative, accept responsibility and carry the weight of accountability before God.

When it came to being a servant according to the Bible, what was it asking me to be? Biblical servant hood allows me to show respect, be willing, loving, self-sacrificing, and submissive. Servant hood didn't mean that I didn't have my own thoughts; just obedient. What it did mean was that I had a willingness to lower myself, to humbly serve another person, and I was able to put the best interests of someone else above my own enjoyment.

ROLE UNDERSTANDING

As a single man, men need to show people of all ages and both sexes that he cares about others, not just himself. He must model a life that is worth following (1 timothy 4:12-16). Single women should be attracted to him because of his character, stability, and desire to edify others.

As a husband, it said for me to be the head of my wife as Christ is the head of the church. I am to love my wife as Christ loved the church (Ephesians 5:23-25). A husband must visibly and verbally put love into action if he expects his wife to be willing to follow his lead.

The father is responsible for the training of his children (Deuteronomy 6:6-9; Ephesians 6:4), and he is to provide for their needs (1 Timothy 5:8), as well as to treat them in a way that doest not exasperate them (Ephesians 6:4; Colossians 3:21).

As a church leader, men in leadership in the church must lead the people under their care, much as a shepherd leads, feeds, protects, and nurtures a flock of sheep (1 Peter 5:1-4). Lastly, is the area of being a member of society. The Old Testament character Daniel demonstrated a willingness to take a stand for the Lord. He did what was right, no matter what the personal risk (Daniel 1, 6). He made a difference because he courageously honored the Lord in a pagan world.

GETTING YOUR HOUSE IN ORDER SERMON

After reviewing a Sunday school lesson entitled "Repent and Return to God (Zechariah 1; 1-6, 7:8-14), I found that it is of great importance that we find ourselves repenting to God and then allowing righteousness to follow our repentance. I needed to repent to God for not being a good steward over all that He had entrusted within my hands, during my lifetime.

My sermon was entitled "Get Your House in Order". I found that in order for a person to be able to do such a thing, one must first come to the realization that something is wrong in their house (spiritually and naturally). You can't make a change if you first don't realize that there is something wrong in your house.

I told the congregation that if they liked the title of the message, they first needed to hold on until they had heard the whole story. I found this message to be important to me first because I was the messenger for that day. I found that as a "Man of God", I needed to have my house in order spiritually, financially and that my family must be directed by me through God. So in saying that, I said this, "Take heed and search your whole house and not just one section of it, but the entire house needs to be in order".

In order to repent, it meant that one must have a change of heart, mind, and behavior so that your actions are different as a result of conviction. Repentance is granted through God's mercy; it is not initiated by man (Acts 11:18). Although it is mans responsibility to repent, he must respond to God's conviction upon his heart. As it was in the days of Zechariah, so also is it now. If repentance does not come through conviction, God will chasten His children until they realize their evil ways and correct them.

I found that in that particular book, the first book of Samuel, Samuel not only anointed both Saul and David, Israel's first two kings, but he also gave definition to the ***new order*** of God's rule over Israel that began with the incorporation of kingship into its structure.

It was also evident that in order for there to have been a new order of God's rule over Israel, there first must have had to be an old way of ruling Israel. If we look at history we can find that the people of Israel were to be led by priests and judges. They saw other nations being ruled by kings, so they demanded a king for themselves later. We have to be careful for what we ask for because we just might get it. We too sometimes ask for things that we are fully ready to receive and be responsible for such as a wife, children, home and a car.

What the children of Israel wanted most was a king instead of a judge. Their judges were charged with maintaining justice, promoting righteousness, and operating generally through a structure or procedure of adjudication in a society. In my research I found out that Moses was the first national judge of God's law, and he appointed godly officials to interpret and apply God's law in daily life of the wilderness. God also gave the high priest a particular right of judgment and the Urim and Thummmim as a way to guide the priest as a judge (Exodus 28:30).

I said all of that to say this, "Something was wrong in the house and the house had to be gotten in order". Is your house all out of whack and how do you know? If it is, then **"Get your house in order"**. What do I mean by your house, I'm glad you asked that question?

House – 1: a building for human habitation 2: a building in which something is stored 3: household; also: family 4: a residence for a religious community or for students.

Order – 1: arrangement, sequence; also: the prevailing state of things 2: a specific rule, regulation, or authoritative direction 3: condition with regard to repair.

In order – 1: appropriate, desirable 2: for the purpose of.

In order to get your house in order one must recognize a few things. I want to first inform you that we will be looking at two different houses and how each person dealt with what was going on in their particular houses.

You must recognize that there is something wrong in your house.

I Samuel 1:15-28

1 Now there was a certain man of Ramthaim-zophim, of mount Ephraim, and his name was Elanah, the son of Heroham, the son of Elihu, the son of Tohu, the son of Zuph an Ephrathite:

2 And he had two wives; the name of the one was Hannah, and the name of the other Peninnah: and Pehninnah had children, but Hannah had no children.

6 And her adversary also provoked her sore, for to make her fret, because the Lord had shut up her womb.

7 And as he did so year by year, when she went up to the house of the Lord, so she provoked her; therefore she wept, and did not eat. (Has your house ever been so tore up that all you knew to do was just cry?)

8 Then said Elkanah her husband to her, Hannah, why weepest thou? And why eatest thou not? And why is thy heart grieved? Am not I better to thee than ten sons? (Sometimes those in your house just don't understand what is really going on within your house; within your spirit man.)

9 So Hannah rose up after they had eaten in Shiloh, and after they had drunk. Now Eli the priest sat upon a seat by a post of the temple of the Lord.

10 And she was in bitterness of soul, and prayed unto the Lord, and wept sore.

You Must Pour Out Your Soul to the Lord (vs. 15).

1 Samuel 1:15

15 And Hannah answered and said, No, my lord, I am a woman of a sorrowful spirit: I have drunk neither wine nor strong drink, but have poured out my soul before the Lord.

Here we find a woman named Hannah realizing that something was wrong in her house. The problem was she was without child. Hannah is an excellent biblical example of one asking God for something in faith. She had married a man named Elkanah and he had other wives. Through the years, Elkanah;s second wife, Peninnah, bore several sons and daughters to him, while Hannah remained barren. Hannah longed for a baby of her own.

Finally, one year Hannah went to the doorway of the tabernacle and wept and ***prayed to the Lord in great anguish***, asking for a son and ***vowing to give him to the Lord***. The Lord heard Hannah's request and answered it. Nine months later she bore a son name Samuel, who grew up to become the prophet and judge of all Israel.

You Must Find Peace and Live in it (vs. 18).

Just as Hannah did, sometimes in life, you have to leave behind your grief. Not when your circumstances change, because sometimes they may not; hers didn't, until after she poured out her soul to the Lord. Because of her grief, ***she connected with the Lord on a level she had never known***. You have to reach God from the depths of your soul. You have to know how to release everything that is holding you back from being all the Lord wants you to be and lay it at His feet. Then and then only will you find peace and be able to live in it.

You Must Then Give Back to God,
What He has Given You (vs. 26-28).

1 Samuel 1:26-28

26 And she said, O my lord, as thy soul liveth, my lord, I am the woman that stood by thee here, praying unto the Lord.

27 For this child I prayed; and the Lord hath given me my petition which I asked of him:

28 Therefore also I have lent him to the Lord; as long as he liveth he shall be lent to the Lord. And he worshipped the Lord there.
Here, the phrase, "as thy soul liveth", was a customary way of emphasizing the <u>truthfulness</u> of one's word. You must keep your promise to God when you have given it to him. The world has a saying, "Your word is your bond or it should be" or "You're only as good as your word". Whatever you vowed, remember this phrase; "A vow may be made by man but it is heard by God". God heard it when it came out of "your mouth" and He expects you to keep your word to Him and others. If you don't mean it when you say it, then don't make or say it in the first place. Remember a liar shall not tarry in His sight!!!

If you have been following the scenario carefully you should have been able to pick up one very familiar trend to this story. Many people know how to run your house, but they can't seem to know what is going on in theirs. Here we will see a classic example of this using the same priest that had a nerve to speak to Hannah concerning her situation. He was so caught up in what he thought was wrong with her that he couldn't see past his front nose; at his own house.

2. Eli's House

2 Samuel 2:22

22 Now Eli was very old, and heard all that his sons did unto all Israel; and how they lay with the women that assembled at the door of the tabernacle of the congregation.

23 and he said unto them, why do ye such things? For I hear of your

evil dealings by all this people.

24 Nay my sons; for it is no good report that I hear: ye make the Lord's people to transgress.

25 If one man sin against another, the judge shall judge him: but if a man sin against the Lord, who shall intreat for him? Notwithstanding they hearkened not unto the voice of their father, because the Lord would slay them.

When you don't find yourself having your house being in order, you may find yourself with a prophecy of doom liken unto Eli. Eli heard "everything that his wicked sons had been doing", **but he took no action**, other than to **mildly rebuke them**.

We should never allow our love for our children to keep us from disciplining them as God directs. We must run our houses as God intended for them to be run; according to the scriptures.

Here are some of life's lessons to be learned here; spiritual privileges bring responsibilities and obligations; they are not to be treated as irrevocable rights.

- Know what is going on in your own house (Take care of business).
- Warning comes before a fall.
- When the warning comes, respond.
- When judgment comes, remember you were warned. This might be your warning right now. Get it right before judgment is pronounced on your house; for tomorrow might be too late.

In closing remember these final scriptures;

1 Samuel 3:11-14

11 And the Lord said to Samuel, Behold, I will do a thing in Israel, at which both the ears of every one that heareth it shall tingle.

12 In that day I will perform against Eli all things which I have spoken concerning his house: when I begin, I will also make an end.

13 For have told him that I will judge his house for ever for the iniquity which he knoweth; because his sons made themselves vile, and he restrained them not.

14 And therefore I have sworn unto the house of Eli, that the iniquity of Eli's house shall not be purged with sacrifice nor offering for ever. NOTE: Don't be like Eli, arrogant and uncaring, and say within yourselves, "It is the Lord: let him do what seemeth him good", because He will.

In chapter 4:18 you will find the demise of Eli, which was death. Because Eli was incapable of restraining Israel or his sons from their wicked ways, and being weakened and blinded by old age, the old priest is an apt symbol of the flawed age now coming to its tragic close. We too have to be careful because we too can be blinded and weakened by the things that are going on in our own houses. Remember, "Get Your House in Order, before the Lord has to do it for you".

Throughout this sermon we should have learned that righteousness must follow repentance. If it doesn't, as in Eli's case, it will result in death. The change in heart must produce a change in behavior. It is not enough to repeatedly ask for forgiveness without first resolving that we are dead to the old man and his ways and that sin no longer has dominion over us.

"I am crucified with Christ: nevertheless I live; yet not I, but Christ liveth in me: and the life which I now live in the flesh I live by the faith of the Son of God, who love me, and gave himself or me (Galatians 2:20). Outwardly, we are perishing, not just physically aging but losing control over our live, but "the inward man is renewed day by day" (2 Corinthians 4:16) as we sow to our spirit and receive renewed strength.

One last departing piece of advice that I want to leave with you, the reader is what Isaiah said in the book of Isaiah 1: 17-20:

17 Learn to do well: seek judgment, relieve the oppressed, judge the fatherless, plead for the widow.

18 Come now, and let us reason together, saith the LORD: though your sins be as scarlet, they shall be as white as snow; though they shall be red like crimson, they shall be as wool.

19 If ye be willing and obedient, ye shall eat of the land:

20 But if ye refuse and rebel, ye shall be devoured with the sword: for the mouth of the LORD hath spoken it.

In this life, we don't have to learn how to evil or be irresponsible, it comes by nature. What we do have to learn is **how to do well.** If this life we have to be able to settle our differences within ourselves. As it pertains to other people being responsible towards us, we must settle the differences or put the matter right that is between us. Such reasoning as this is where all parties that are concerned can state their own cases. This alone will put an end to all other reasoning and questionings. The hope is that the sinner will see his need and give himself to God and then God will be just in cleansing him from all sin and make him His son. Remember the responsibility is yours for the accepting. Will you do it today?

End Notes

A.W. Pink

(Source: Digestive Diseases in the United States: Epidemiology and Impact, National Digestive Diseases Data Working Group, James E. Everhart, MD, MPH, Editor, US Department of Health and Human Services, Public Health Service, National Institutes of Health, NIH Publication No. 94-1447, May 1994)

Merriam-Webster, Incorporated
Springfield, Massachusetts, U.S.A.
Copyright 2000 by Merriam-Webster, Incorporated

Unless otherwise noted, Scripture quotations are from the Holy Bible, New International Version, copyright 1973, 1978, 1978, 1984 by International Bible Society. Used by permission of Zondervan Publishing House.

Battlefield of the Mind
Winning the Battle in Your Mind
ISBN 1- 57794 - 169 - 1
(Formerly ISBN 0-89274 - 778 -1)
Copyright 1995 by Joyce Meyer
Life in The Word, Inc.
P.O. Box 655
Fenton, Missouri 63026
Published by Harrison House Inc., P.O. Box 35035, Tulsa, Oklahoma 74153

Davis, RV: Therapeutic Modalities for the Clinical Health Sciences, 1st ed., 1983. Copyright -- Library of Congress Card # TXU-389-661.

Griffin JE, Karselis TC: Physical Agents for Physical Therapists, 2nd ed. Springfield: Charles C. Thomas 1982.

Hoppenfield: Physical Examination of the Spine & Extremities, 2nd ed. New York: Appleton/Century/Craft.

Krusen, Kottke, Ellwood: Handbook of Physical Medicine & Rehabilitation, 2nd ed. Philadelphia: W.B. Saunders Company, 1971.

Schriber WA: A Manual of Electrotherapy, 4th ed. Philadelphia: Lea & Feibiger, 1975.

Turek: Orthopedics -- Their Principles and Applications, 3rd ed. Lippincott Publishers.